SUNNY'S NIGHTS

SUNNY'S NIGHTS

*Lost and Found at a Bar
on the Edge of the World*

TIM
SULTAN

Random House | New York

Published in the United States by Random House, an imprint and division of
Penguin Random House LLC, New York.

RANDOM HOUSE and the HOUSE colophon are registered trademarks of
Penguin Random House LLC.

Grateful acknowledgment is made to Hal Leonard Corporation for permission
to reprint an excerpt from "Rainy Night in Georgia," words and music by Tony
Joe White, copyright © 1969 (renewed 1997) by TEMI Combine Inc. All rights
controlled by Combine Music Corp. and administered by EMI Blackwood
Music Inc. Excerpt from "Walk on the Wild Side," words and music by Lou
Reed, copyright © 1972 by Oakfield Avenue Music Ltd. All rights controlled and
administered by EMI Music Publishing Ltd. All rights reserved. International
Copyright Secured. Used by permission of Hal Leonard Corporation.

Photograph on page 70 courtesy of Antonio Balzano. Photograph
on page 99 © De Agostini Picture Library/Getty Images. Photograph on page
181 courtesy of Jason Elias.

LIBRARY OF CONGRESS CATALOGING-IN-PUBLICATION DATA
Sultan, Tim.
Sunny's nights : lost and found at a bar on the edge of the world / by Tim Sultan.
pages cm
ISBN 978-1-4000-6727-5 — ISBN 978-0-8129-8848-2 (ebook)
1. Sultan, Tim.   2. Bartenders—New York (State)—New York—Biography.
3. Bartending—New York (State)—New York.   4. Red Hook (N.Y.)—
Social life and customs.   5. Brooklyn (New York, N.Y.)—Social life and
customs.   I. Title.
TX950.5.S85S85 2016
641.87'409747—dc23
2015019985

Printed in the United States of America on acid-free paper

randomhousebooks.com

2 4 6 8 9 7 5 3 1

First Edition

Book design by Susan Turner

In memory of my parents, Herbert and Ursula

SUNNY'S NIGHTS

1

Antonio

THERE IS A CORNER TURNED, A DIRECTION TAKEN. There is a door opened in everyone's history that they can identify as the moment life, for better or worse, took a different course. Eve bit an apple. Dante saw Beatrice. Jack met Neal. For me, that corner, that direction, that door appeared late in the winter of 1995. The place was Red Hook, Brooklyn, the hour late, the mood desolate. I had gone to the night's last showing of Woody Allen's *Bullets Over Broadway* and while driving home from the theater, mulling over the movie, I had half-absentmindedly continued straight where I usually took a left, slipping beneath an overpass and entering a neighborhood I knew only by its forbidding reputation. There were no other cars and no people and long stretches of shadow between the streetlamps. I drove on. Deliberately getting lost had been a pastime of mine since early childhood. I was raised by parents who only asked that I be home before sundown. By adolescence, I had lost my bearings in Laotian rice paddies, German forests, and a West African city where the practice of naming streets had not yet been widely adopted. In college one autumn, I courted a woman by inventing a game in which one of us would close our eyes and pretend to be blind, while the other made believe they were mute, and the mute person would lead the blind one by the hand on late-evening ambles through professors' backyards and frosty Ohio pastures. By winter, we could have written dissertations on the merits of disorientation but we merely fell in love instead.

That Friday night in Red Hook I was twenty-seven years old, and again I found myself taking left and right turns seemingly at random, unsure whether I was sightseeing or soul-searching. A succession of low-slung industrial warehouses and towering fuel tanks gave way to darkened fields and from them the silhouette of an enormous building rose up, as still and monstrous as a pyramid. Bare trees bordering the road were the only living beings in sight. More turns. The pavement soon gave way to cobblestones and I slowed the car to a walking pace. Another building, vaguely Georgian, came into view. Its doorways and arched windows were sealed with bricks giving it the look of an asylum or prison or school, irrevocably shuttered. I deciphered white letters near the top: *Shipyards Corporation*.

Other lone structures appeared and melted away in my headlamps. I continued straight until I could go straight no farther. I had come to another corner. *Conover Street*, read the sign. Ahead, behind a rusty gate, stretched a barren lot and beyond that the water of the harbor shimmered faintly. To my right stood several satellite dishes, so immense they seemed capable of beaming their messages not only to New

Jersey but to new planets. To the left more signs appeared in the gloom, one profoundly weird (*Animal Hair Manufacturing Company*) and the other weirdly spare (*Bar*). I pulled over and turned off the engine. I looked up and down the cobblestone street. There was no movement, no sound. I was alone and the sense of solitude that descended on me was as absolute as that usually only found in dreams. I wavered but a few moments before getting out of my car. Where bars were concerned, my spirit of inquiry always seemed to prevail over a sense of caution. I paused at the first building. *Animal Hair Manufacturing Company*. What could it mean? I walked on toward the next sign. *Bar*. I knew of a bar called the No Name Bar but I had never seen a bar that literally had no name. I had come to a place, it seemed, where the world was returning to its most elemental properties.

I took a few more tentative steps until I stood beneath one of two faded brown awnings. In between was a simple wooden door containing three peephole windows ascending from left to right as though to accommodate lookouts of varying heights. Two more storefront windows on either side of the door emanated a faint light and in this glow I could see a wooden ship and a black-and-white photograph of a sailor from an earlier generation resting on a ledge inside. The picture might have been taken during the Second World War.

I considered the forlornness of the area and of the night. I had entered a lot of bars in my life and rarely with hesitation. An early bloomer of a sort, I had my first tavern beer at fourteen and I graduated high school with the inglorious honor of being voted by my classmates as the student most likely to be found not in a bar—that distinction went to my best friend—but under a bar. While I had gotten dissipation out of my system by the time I was an adult, I still knew my way around bars in the way a person raised on a farm never forgets how to cross a livestock yard. I reached forward and pulled open the door and stepped inside. Every one of the two dozen faces in the room was turned toward me. Pale faces, male faces, their attention to my entrance so complete, I might as well have burst into act I, scene 2 at the Delacorte. It was too late to turn around and exit stage left without feeling the fool. And so, I let the door softly close behind me.

In the brief time it took for my eyes to adjust to the dim light, I realized that the collective gaze was directed not at me but a movie screen that hung to the left of the door. A projector hummed in the rear of the room, its beam cutting through the gloom like a locomotive headlight. On the screen, opening credits were just beginning to appear. Martha Graham. Aaron Copland. Isamu Noguchi. Soon dancers in pioneer dress were swirling in black and white. Tinny classical music played. To the right, stools lined the bar. I slid onto the third one in and swiveled toward the screen. Among the several scenarios I'd considered moments before as I had paused on the stoop outside—most involving a roomful of repeat offenders as glad to see me as their parole officers—a collection of men quietly smoking and watching a classic of modern dance had not been one of them. Encouraged, I waved to a figure leaning back against a counter behind the bar and, in a low voice, asked for a beer.

"How about a Rheingold?" whispered the shadowy form.

"Sure. Rheingold," I replied, and returned to the dancers.

My neighbors up and down the length of the bar and dotting the room were as absorbed by the show as an orchestra-row audience. Following suit, I, too, let myself be drawn in to the story of newlyweds starting out life on the American frontier. *Appalachian Spring,* like all of Copland's cheery music, had always had the approximate effect on me of sour milk, but after a few minutes I decided that beer and a crude sound system improved him. Ballet, too, was made more tolerable when observed from a barstool. The pangs of torment I usually began to feel at such performances didn't begin to set in even as I watched for a good twenty minutes. After the screen at last went dark, a middle-aged, bookish-looking man with a trimmed white beard and glasses quickly began exchanging reels. Before anyone had much chance to stir, the projector started up again and we were watching a documentary on Brooklyn bakeries that was narrated with the earnestness of a middle-school social studies film on the catacombs of Rome and appeared to have been made around the last time a general was president of the United States. As bread baked and yeast rose, seemingly in real time, I wondered a little where this night was headed. Not two hours earlier I had been sitting in an ordinary movie theater in a familiar part of town, taking in a light crime caper with a bucket of popcorn in my lap. Now I found myself in the dark of an entirely different kind of theater, one where the program seemed to have been chosen with the help of a roulette wheel. By the time the next selection, an abstract short by Stan Brakhage made with moth wings and leaves, was under way, I began to speculate whether there wasn't a method to the madness. Ballet, bakeries, Brakhage—if we remained in our seats long enough, would we eventually move on to cabalism, calligraphy, Caligula . . .

But the final movies of the night were several silent cityscapes of 1970s New York, shot, our curator explained between reels, when he was with a girl who had a peyote habit. The girl appeared several times, sitting mutely on a couch, as the camera swung from one window to another, each a framed portrait of the city skyline.

The whirring projector stopped for good and a few yellow lights were turned on. I gestured down the bar for another round. As I waited for my beer and gazed around the room, a spindly, hollow-eyed man with a guitar in hand suddenly stood up and announced he was going to sing a song he had written in a Texas basement. His voice was resolutely unmusical and his guitar playing paid a debt to clanging radiators but the song's refrain would have made greater and lesser poets despair with envy: "She's not a vixen, she voted for Richard Nixon." What a line!

I sat on the stool, twirling my now empty bottle, taking it all in.

The films. The singer. The nautical farrago that cluttered the walls and shelves. The trio of coffee urns the size of fire hydrants near the front door, the Blatz Beer boiled-egg dispenser, the plaster mannequins of stars of the silver screen—Bogart, Fields, Durante, Marx (Groucho), West, Marx (Harpo)—mingling in various corners. The bar counter was charred in places where cigarettes had been stubbed out. A painting of a horse hung on one wall in a spot where over time just enough sunlight must have fallen to bleach the head out: a headless horse in a nameless bar. A hook, which looked as though it once served as someone's prosthetic hand, dangled from a chain of Christmas lights. And high above the bar sat several model ships in glass cases. There were no pinball chimes, no televisions turned to hockey, no machines at all (other than the projector and the stereo tucked somewhere behind the counter on which Julie London was now singing). The letters *Avenue P* pointed the way to the bathroom, but there was no signage that would give away the year or the decade we were in. Only the clothes of the customers revealed the era, and then only fitfully. The bar looked old and worn but not in the overly careful manner of certain New York saloons where amber beer seems to take on a whole new meaning.

My eyes came to rest on the barkeep. He was laughing, chatting, smoking as he made his way along his side of the bar with my next Rheingold. From a distance, he looked vaguely Native American, like Chief Dan George of *Little Big Man* fame. But he also resembled Tony Bennett, if Tony Bennett had last seen a barber in 1957. Up close, I decided that if one took Tiny Tim's hair and put it on Gertrude Stein's face, one would get a very good likeness of this man. From what little I had heard of his voice, he sounded kind of Irish, but when my beer arrived and I introduced myself, he said, "My real name is Antonio. Antonio Raffaele Balzano. But please. Call me Sunny." He gripped my hand in both of his and leaned across the bar.

He was tall and very slim but the features on his face were large and rounded as a ship's weathered figurehead. His eyebrows were two silver caterpillars that had come to a halt while walking Indian file across his brow. His fingers were as thick as a stout woman's wrists. In the shadows, he had appeared a little otherworldly and a little epicene—less the ghost of the Ancient Mariner than that of the Mariner's sister. But now he grasped my hand with the vigor and enthusiasm and curiosity of a man coming upon a compatriot after months lost in the jungle. It was a greeting startling in its sincerity and intensity, and one that I would come to see made to others many times. It expressed: "You belong." To say that he exuded charisma would be like saying Mussolini liked to hear himself talk.

ANTONIO—SUNNY—EVENTUALLY continued on, stopping to speak with each person or party seated at the bar. I watched him and I watched how everyone else kept an eye on him, as if awaiting a turn to be in his company. He kept a cigarette continuously lit and often tilted his head back to blow plumes of smoke in the air. He sipped whiskey out of shot glasses that looked like thimbles in his hands while telling stories about rats he had slain at various times in his life. Though I only heard snatches, I assumed he meant the kind with whiskers and tails. He recited several lines of what I took to be Shakespeare. He pronounced words in a way I had never heard before. He might say, "I ate a plate of ersters and then I slipped on some erl on my way to the terlet." He used strange words rarely heard in casual conversation, like "verbiage" and "personage." And he used words strangely, saying for instance, "Within the framework that it is that it is that we're existing in."

I was certain that I had never encountered a more arresting presence.

I stayed awhile longer in the hope Sunny would come back over to where I was sitting but he was so deeply engrossed in conversation that eventually, I put my jacket and cap on and slipped out the door as quietly as I had come in, knowing I would be back.

But the next time I returned—and the one or two times after that—I found the bar dark, the door locked, the street deserted. I cupped my face against the window and peered into the inkiness inside, but there was no sign of Sunny, of the projector's flicker, or of any of the drinking, smoking men who had been there that first night. The sailor in the photograph in the window was the only witness who could corroborate that the night had taken place at all.

Months passed, until one evening in September I was returning from a quiet dinner with a onetime flame in Manhattan and feeling that restive curiosity again. I decided to give Sunny and his bar one more try. I slowly drove down his block and as I passed the two shabby awnings, I thought I could detect a glow coming from inside. I parked by the Animal Hair Manufacturing Company. I walked to the front door and I saw that the colored Christmas lights strung up behind the bar were lit again and I entered and sat at the same spot, three rickety barstools in. Many of the same faces were there. When Sunny saw me, he strolled over, cried, "Timmy! How are you, my buddy?" and leaned across the bar to embrace me.

"You remember my name?"

"Of course I do. How could I not?"

And so our friendship began.

2

Divine Athambia

I soon learned that this bar of Sunny's, the bar with no name and therefore no listing in the phone book, had been in his family since the beginning and he himself had practically been born there. I also learned that it was only open every seventh day, like a roadhouse in the Old Testament. This struck me as less than sound business practice, but the business of running a bar did not appear to be the business that Sunny was in. I couldn't remember ever meeting someone so free of worry about making money, about rules, about doing things in the accustomed way. I noticed that Sunny carried a remarkably spare stock—a few staples, Romanian vodka, peach and blackberry brandies. Wino liquor. He served wine from cartons, strongly reminiscent of communion wine (though any priest serving Holy Communion with this stuff would quickly have a dwindling parish on his hands). Although there were vestiges of taps, there was no actual draft beer to be had; Sunny explained that he opened too infrequently to keep it fresh. If one was nevertheless dead set on having a beer, he leisurely reached behind him into a wooden cooler built into the back counter, not overly concerned whether it was Budweiser, Rheingold, Heineken, or Schlitz that he fished out. All beers—all drinks, for that matter—were three dollars at Sunny's. He showed even less concern if a customer, impatient for service, came around the bar and simply helped himself.

Sunny was not in the least proprietary, at least not overtly. If a person expressed admiration or fidelity to his bar, he would say, "My bar? This isn't my bar any more than it's anyone else's bar. It don't belong to me. It belongs to each of you who have come here and have served to make it what it is that it is. It's our bar, aye?" He appeared to mean this in the most sincere way. It was an outlook that emboldened customers to make whatever contribution to the humanities they wished. There weren't always obscure films being projected or ingenious songs being sung, though a bakery-truck driver with a guitar and a Maine accent thicker than Edmund Muskie's usually got up once a Friday and sang of his Long Island route, "You can have it all / Any way you like / You can have it all / On the Jericho Turnpike!"—perhaps the most hopeful sentiment about a stretch of road since Nat King Cole first crooned, "You can get your kicks / On Route 66."

There was a sense that one was off the leash here. The culture that I came upon at Sunny's was a distinct and self-generated one, as you might expect to find on an island far from any shore. If a stocky biker named Ross wanted to stand in the middle of the room and play two trumpets simultaneously, sounding less like Rahsaan Roland Kirk than a subway car's brakes thirsting for oil, Sunny was unperturbed. If a chauffeur wanted to noisily recite Harold Pinter ("You have a wonderful casserole . . . I mean wife"), Sunny was appreciative. If the rare woman patron, and an adult entertainer no less, wanted to perform an interpretive dance of Aphrodite's birth wearing something less than pasties, Sunny was understanding. And if a tugboat captain, addressed as Captain Ritchie both on and off the water, decided abruptly to yodel, and yodel very ably at that, Sunny loved it. He loved it because he seemed to love people in an absolutist manner that I had rarely seen. His affection for them, his curiosity about their histories, and his appreciation for their customs and eccentricities were apparent in the way he engaged his patrons and in his habit of extolling their virtues and their vices. He particularly loved vices. He always seemed to be exalting people, whether to their faces, behind their backs, or, as he often did, indirectly while telling a story.

One night in those first few months at the bar, Sunny, looking into the middle distance, had begun reciting Lucky's monologue from *Waiting for Godot* (he had, I would learn, an intense interest in theater). "Given the existence as uttered forth in the public works of Puncher and Wattmann," he intoned, "of a personal God quaquaquaqua with white beard quaquaquaqua outside time without extension who from the heights of divine apathia divine athambia divine aphasia loves us dearly with some exceptions . . ." And a customer, conceivably better acquainted with Ireland's whiskey than its playwrights, confused as to why Sunny was now referring to himself as Lucky, asked, "Well, which is it now? Sunny or Lucky?"

"Can't I be both?"

"I don't know," said the man, an elderly widower named

Frankie Brown who drove over regularly from Staten Island, mostly for the company since he always brought his own beer. "I've seen the kind of attention you get from women so you might say you're lucky in love. How 'bout cards? You lucky in cards?"

"I might play the lotto now and then," Sunny replied. "And I like to gamble in the sense that I take chances in life but I don't really gamble in the conventional sense that it is you're referring to."

Frankie Brown blinked at Sunny and seemed to be searching his mind for another explanation as to why Sunny might be calling himself lucky.

"Although now that you mention it, I do remember this one time," Sunny continued after pausing on his cigarette. "I was traveling cross-country with a friend of mine and we stopped in Reno. He had to make some calls so I said, 'I'll call home.' I put the kern in the phone and it spits out like two, three bucks. I put another kern in the phone and out comes more money. I was playing the phones! That was my Reno gambling experience. I played the phones and I came out ahead."

"Well, so you really are lucky," said Frankie, brightening. "Lucky Balzano. Lucky like Luciano. You oughtta make a phone call more often."

"Nye, the truth of the matter is that I am probably the unluckiest gambler that there ever has been," Sunny said. "I am the gambler that has known the near miss."

"How you mean, Sunny?" Frankie asked. (As I would very soon figure out for myself, "How you mean, Sunny?" was the sort of thing one asked when one had plenty of time on one's hands.)

"Well, I'll tell you why. There was this friend of mine. You may remember him, Frankie, because his name was Frankie, too, only you're Frankie Brown and this Frankie they called 'Blackjack' because he'd be in a bar and a fight would break out and he'd pull out a blackjack and conk people over the head with it.

"Anyway, Frankie liked to take me to Atlantic City every once in a while. As I said, I never was much of a gambler and I went really just to give him company. He used to be with a girl named Mary Ann who lived around the corner and when I'd go over to his house to pick him up, he would shout up the stairs as we were leaving, 'MARY ANN. WE'RE GOING TO GO. WE'LL SEE YOU IN A COUPLE OF WEEKS!' Because our intention was that if we won, we were going to stay. We were going to stay until we'd used up all of the money.

"So this one time, we got into the casino and there's a wall there with slot machines and there's a wall here. Catty-corner. Now, Frankie's working a machine on one side and I'm sitting over by the other wall and the others are mostly taken. Meantime, I didn't know that I could use two slot machines at once. And I say, 'Frankie, can I use this?' And he says, 'Yeah, you can use as many as you want.' I say, 'Why don't you come over and use this one?' and I pernt to the one next to me. And he says, 'But I'm hitting, Sunny. I'm doin' okay. You go ahead and play it.' We were playing dollar chips. So, I'm putting chips here and I'm putting chips there and this woman comes over with a group of her friends. Elderly. She says to me, 'Are you using this machine?' and pernts to the machine next to where I'm sitting—the machine I had invited Frankie to play. So I say, 'I am but you can use it if you like.'

And son of a bitch, she sticks in her kern and fuckin' bells start going! I didn't know what the hell was happening. Frankie didn't know what was happening. He might'a thought it was me. She hit the jackpot! I think it was eighty-four thousand dollars. The guards come and do the whole thing that they do and she walks away and turns to me and says, 'Thank you' and waves. One kern away from the jackpot! 'WE'LL SEE YOU IN A COUPLE OF WEEKS!' That one time, that one time we came close to those couple of weeks. So, no. Not Lucky. You better just call me Sunny."

Sunny was equally at home speaking Beckettese and Brooklynese. In his gravelly voice, he enunciated words with a *Masterpiece Theatre* formality that made one think of John Gielgud or William F. Buckley introducing an episode of *Brideshead Revisited,* while also allowing several "fuhgeddaboudits" into every half-hour of conversation—though when he did so, he was no more aware that he was engaging in vernacularism than a French bulldog is aware of being French.

Indeed, he seemed to be unsuspecting that there was anything remarkable about himself at all.

3

The Last Small Town
in New York City

THE RED HOOK I'D FOUND MYSELF IN THAT FIRST
night at Sunny's was a ghost town. Not in the way of a
forsaken mining town in the Southwest, more like the abandoned vicinities of former industrial cities: Baltimore, Sche-
nectady, Cleveland, Flint—places where industry boomed,
industry died, and the people that served that industry have
vanished. Had one taken a man from 1854, when Red Hook
had one of the great settlements of the Irish in Brooklyn, or
1884, when the expansion of the largest dry dock in the country had just been completed there, or 1934, the year of Sunny's birth, and deposited him on the corner of any two streets
along the Red Hook waterfront in 1994, he would have looked
around and asked, "Where'd everyone go?"

Where dockworkers had once crowded shape-ups, where
labor racketeers had ruled, where bounty hoppers hid, boot-

leggers distilled, arsonists lit, nuns crossed, longshoremen hauled, unions agitated, kids pelted, gangs brawled, it was now so quiet you could hear the bell buoys in the harbor clanging like church bells calling truant parishioners. Brick warehouses dating to Reconstruction, and some row and frame houses older still, stood amidst empty grassy lots, but there were no restaurants, no bars. There was Sunny's place and a VFW post and a few small sandwich shops and bodegas. Most of the population that remained was clustered in a sprawling public housing project on the eastern side of the neighborhood, an area known locally as "the Front" to distinguish it from the waterfront quarter around Sunny's, which was referred to as "the Back." It was a division that dated to the previous century, long before such a thing as public housing existed, when the boundary line was said to follow the path of a creek. Though the creek eventually dried up and the bed was paved over and became a street, the border remained, now delineated in asphalt.

I knew nothing then about this unofficial partition of the neighborhood, but I did already know about invisible boundaries. Since moving to New York in 1991, I had lived in Park Slope, a leafy neighborhood of fin de siècle brownstones just minutes away by car, but I had only dimly been aware of Red Hook in all that time. Surrounded on three sides by water and on the fourth by an expressway, the neighborhood was isolated and strangely remote. It was a corner of the city that rarely made the news. And when it did, it was mostly in connection with crime, tragedy, or municipal neglect. Red Hook was where the local elementary school principal was shot and killed while out looking for an absentee student a couple years earlier. It was where the previous summer a turf soccer field—donated by the government of Norway to coincide with the World Cup—was set on fire by teenagers days after being installed. At the time, a city official simply mocked the Scandinavians' naiveté for putting their field in Red Hook. "Red Hook isn't Norway."

Red Hook was notorious. A place to take garbage and corpses. Dead Hook. At least that had been my own very vague sense of the place before coming to Sunny's: hearsay and gangster mythology. *Wasn't that where Al Capone earned the nickname Scarface? Didn't* On the Waterfront *have something to do with Red Hook? Isn't that where Joey Gallo kept a lion in his basement?*

AT ONE TIME, the name "Red Hook" had encompassed a far larger neighborhood, stretching north to Atlantic Avenue and the edge of Brooklyn Heights and east to the foothills of Park Slope. It was Robert Moses, New York City's unofficial master planner, who, in the 1940s, had an elevated expressway built over what was then the neighborhood's main commercial street, and later connected that expressway with another to its north, creating a river of cars through the center of the old Red Hook and cleaving the harborside half from the rest of the borough of Brooklyn. In his influence on thousands of mid-century Brooklynites, Moses must have seemed more powerful than his ancient namesake, parting not mere water but land.

What now lay to the north and east of this concrete moat soon took on new names—Carroll Gardens, Cobble Hill, and Boerum Hill—as if to disavow any relation to their past

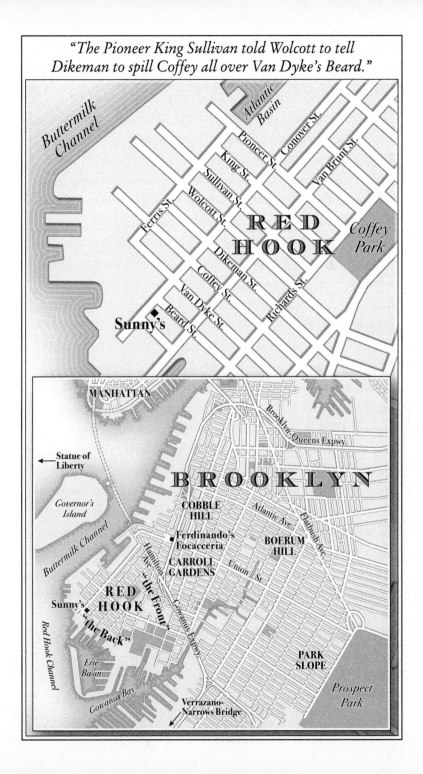

"The Pioneer King Sullivan told Wolcott to tell Dikeman to spill Coffey all over Van Dyke's Beard."

during a time when the word "red" itself was viewed with suspicion.

But for those who lived in the low-lying areas close to the water, there was no escaping "Red Hook." In this area—known at least since the 1880s as Red Hook Point, its inhabitants called Pointers—a sense of separateness, not only from the rest of Brooklyn but from the northern half of the neighborhood, had existed long before Robert Moses rose to prominence. Those who had lived below Hamilton Avenue and closer to the harbor had always held the view that they were the true Red Hookers, while those who lived above this line would just as soon have referred to themselves as living in South Brooklyn or Old Brooklyn. Robert Moses had merely set in stone a border that had already existed between Red Hook Point and greater Brooklyn for generations.

As early as the 1840s, when the first great wave of Irish immigration hit New York, Red Hook Point was thought of as an alien enclave within the city of Brooklyn—though less San Marino than Devil's Island. A home for fugitives, bootleggers, and rumrunners; a vicinity where, in 1842, people were advised to do their marketing during daylight hours so as to avoid the knives of thieves hiding in the marshes. Sensational accounts of bodies found in various states of decomposition in Red Hook's fetid swamps filled the crime blotters of nineteenth-century tabloids, and the hometown newspaper, *The Brooklyn Eagle,* variously described Red Hook Point as "a strange and odious place," "an unknown region," and a place where "some of the worst murders that have ever been recorded took place."

A full half-century before the macabre H. P. Lovecraft

would describe his neighborhood as a cauldron of deviance and iniquity in "The Horror at Red Hook," the *Eagle* wrote:

> There is scarcely a ward in Brooklyn that does not contain within its precincts dens so infamous in their character, and in the character of the inhabitants, that the more respectable portion of the community would start back in horror at the idea of breathing the atmosphere tainted by their proximity. In some immorality, unbridled and unfettered, bears sway; in some thieving and dishonesty prevail, while in others the pallid faces, tattered garments, bleared eyes, and shriveled bodies, bear unerring testimony to the degrading effects of dissipation, and in more than one case can be found the assassin and murderer, ignoring altogether petty crimes as beneath their notice. . . . Red Hook Point stands out in bold relief as being the grand central and amalgamated cesspool and sink of low life in Brooklyn.

If nineteenth-century Red Hook appeared to outsiders to be a vile settlement, twentieth-century Red Hook would become synonymous with criminal gangs, extortionists, black marketeers, skirmishes between the Irish and the Italians, longshoremen's union corruption, and internecine Mafia wars. It was here in 1903 that the Black Hand made its first appearance in America. A now-forgotten phenomenon, the Black Hand was widely believed to be a sinister criminal fraternity, with origins in Sicily, that fanned out from Red Hook across New York and to Italian communities in other cities. Extortion letters and bombings were its calling card.

Newspaper readers were told that the Black Hand was world-wide and that its adherents had arrived on American shores to set up cells and plunder our wealth.

It was in Red Hook, too, that the White Hand, an Irish gang whose territory and source of income were the piers that stretched from the southeastern end of the neighborhood to the Manhattan Bridge, ruled for much of the 1920s. The White Hand specialized in protection rackets, taxation of the docks, and simple theft, in sum an operation that netted enough income to make gang boss a sought-after position. There was one catch to being the White Hand's chief executive officer—one's tenure was sure to be short and one would suffer a violent death at the hands of one's successor. The rise and demise of White Handers such as Dinny Meehan, Peg-Leg Lonergan, Garry Barry, Wild Bill Lovett, Cinders Connolly, Red Donnelly, and the eleven other known heads of the gang were given dramatic coverage in the press. The shortest stint as leader of the White Hand was that of Eddie McGuire, who in 1928 foolishly agreed to roll dice against Red Donnelly for supremacy of the gang. Minutes after McGuire rolled a winning three and four, Donnelly shot him dead on a dark pier.

By 1926, the juvenile delinquency rate in Red Hook was five times greater than that of any other district in Brooklyn and the New York State Crime Commission chose the neighborhood for a study on the causes of crime. Describing Red Hook as "an unusually provincial district tucked away in a large city, with most of its residents neither knowing nor caring about what goes on beyond the section's narrow bounds," the commission concluded that the children's concept of adult life came from "watching the men of Red Hook engage freely in drinking, gambling, brawling, shooting, and stabbing matches."

Robert Moses must have thought he was doing the rest of Brooklyn a favor when he built his expressway and sealed Red Hook away.

My own father, who grew up in Depression-era East New York, Brooklyn, then the home of Murder Inc. killers like Bugsy Goldstein and Mendy Weiss, looked shaken when I told him over dinner where I had begun spending my Friday nights.

"Red Hook!" he exclaimed. "That was no-man's-land when I was a kid. Nobody went to Red Hook!"

No doubt Red Hookers of the time didn't think of themselves as living in a *True Detective* tale or an Elia Kazan movie. But Red Hook was home to enough criminals to fill its own wing of the rogues' gallery. In addition to the White Handers, mob eminences like Frankie Yale, Al Capone, Albert Anastasia and his brother Anthony "Tough Tony" Anastasio, Joey Gallo, and in more recent times, the unsung men and boys who fought territorial battles for the street corners in the shadows of the housing projects, all contributed to the notion of Red Hook as a place of mayhem and thuggery that persisted nearly to this day. Some social commentators wondered whether there wasn't a geographical determinism at work, the very words "red" and "hook" bringing to mind blood passion, butchery, aggression. Impalement by gaff. No self-respecting lowlife would want to admit to being raised in a place called "Park Slope," "Carroll Gardens," or "Windsor Terrace."

Can a sense of criminality linger in a neighborhood like mercury in groundwater? Most New Yorkers would scoff at this. It is the matter-of-fact nature of modern cities to be ever-changing, buildings razed, buildings erected, expressways inserted through the very space once occupied by families sitting down at the dinner table and couples talking in their beds, erasing all but the most notable events and personalities of an era. Many moments in our New York lifetimes, we step on the same pavement where precious life once bled out and we are, of course, unfazed. Nobody now walks along East 108th Street and feels a chill when they pass the spot where Ignazio Lupo was said to keep bodies on meat hooks at his infamous Murder Stable. Coney Island's late Half Moon Hotel, from whose sixth-floor window mob turncoat Abe Reles ("the canary that sang but couldn't fly") took a fatal plunge, is mainly recalled only by the Jewish senior citizens who live in the retirement home that was built in its place. Whoever resides at 152 20th Street in Brooklyn, onetime home to Al Capone's hangout the Adonis Social Club and scene of the 1925 Christmas Day Massacre, presumably does not sense Scarface's spirit there. There are no haunted places in New York because no one can afford depreciating the real estate for such darkly sentimental reasons.

But my new friend Sunny believed karma existed for neighborhoods as surely as for people. Accordingly, Red Hook, in its dereliction, was still suffering the consequences of misdeeds that had taken place long ago. Or, as Sunny would put it, "The residue of these actions is experienced by the children of their children."

There was a more prosaic reason for Red Hook's current state, too: the late ripples of the Industrial Revolution. Containerization in shipping and the automation of the docks eliminated most of the unskilled port jobs by the 1960s, and thirty years later nearly all the remaining maritime industry had moved to Port Newark–Elizabeth in New Jersey. The century-and-a-half-long tide of families that had arrived first from Holland, Ireland, Germany, Portugal, Scandinavia, Italy, and eventually Puerto Rico and the Dominican Republic had come to an end, and when their descendants decamped else-where, following jobs and fleeing circumstances, they left be-hind untended houses and crumbling piers. Nearly all of the eleven thousand people who remained in Red Hook lived in the public housing towers of "The Front," while the few who remained in the homes near the harbor enjoyed a backwater existence scarcely still found in New York. Its inaccessibility, its insularity, the residue of a violent past—whatever the cause, Red Hook was quiet as a neglected cemetery in the spring of 1995 when I arrived. Sunny once described the pro-vincialism of his youth to me by saying, "Red Hook never left Red Hook." But in the present day, the inverse was true— the rest of Brooklyn, the Bronx, Queens, and Manhattan never entered Red Hook and looking across the harbor at Staten Island at night was like looking across the Strait of Gibraltar at the coastline of an unknown continent.

With scant industry, few stores, little traffic—the occa-sional car was usually either being driven by a student driver lurching down the empty streets or being towed to the neigh-borhood's impound lot—much of Red Hook had even been forsaken by the criminals. There was no one left to rob. In-stead of bodies, it was torched cars that were dumped on the cobblestones (the unaccountably beautiful sight of a joyride left ablaze in the middle of an intersection during a snowstorm one night has never left me). The last time anyone at the bar could recall a body being ditched, it had been spotted by a customer smoking his cigar out front. But, in this case, the body was still alive. Beaten and naked, the man ducked and crouched, trying to cover himself as he crept from the unlit dead end of the street toward the glow of the bar windows. When the customers inside learned what had happened they took up a collection of clothes—a shirt, a sweater, socks (no one remembers which selfless souls donated their pants and shoes)—and Sunny called a cab and stuck enough money into the stranger's pocket for the ride back to wherever he came from. In the course of an evening, the wretch experienced the truth of the words of sixth-century Roman philosopher (and hero of mine) Boethius, who wrote of Lady Fortune: "This is the way she amuses herself; this is the way she shows her power. She shows her servants the marvel of a man despairing and happy within the single hour."

The neighborhood was so quiet that Sunny once impulsively bought a Central Park horse carriage with the idea that he would rent a horse and driver when the urge to ride around the neighborhood hit him. This was a typical thing for Sunny to do; he lived life sumptuously though he never had much money.

Sunny never actually got around to hiring a horse. Eventually—and impulsively—Sunny bought a dark green 1951 Jeep Willys that he saw idle and friendless in front of a gas station. For a couple years he even drove it, though rarely more than a quarter mile from the bar and at a speed somewhere between a trot and gallop. Nowadays it is parked permanently out front of the bar, where the cab is used as a smoking room or, when it's raining, as a phone booth.

4

Arcadia

I KNOW NOW THAT I WAS LUCKY TO ARRIVE WHEN I DID—
when Red Hook was still sleepy and beautiful and cut off
from the rest of the world in ways that are hard to imagine
anymore. The rest of the world was where I came from. I
would never actually say this, of course, when asked during
bar conversation. For a time, I simply answered, "I'm from
Park Slope." This didn't always go over very well at Sunny's.
I was informed by one man that the women of Park Slope had
more periods than a Hemingway novel. Another said he had
been to a bar in Park Slope for a drink recently and that he
hadn't slept so well since church.

Eventually, I began telling something closer to the truth.
"I'm from no place."

I had no hometown and I was raised in somewhat nomadic circumstances. By age eleven, I was on my third continent. Born in Bangkok in the fall of 1967, within a week I
boarded a plane with my mother, bound for Laos where my

father, a Foreign Service officer, and three brothers were waiting. Our home was an American enclave outside the capital, Vientiane, a kind of Levittown transplanted to a tropical countryside. I would spend my first seven years there, a montage of paddy and jungle, water buffaloes and elephants, monks and candles, comic books and cookouts, geckos and cobras, dry and rainy seasons, monsoon floods and makeshift boats. I pummeled tethered balls and shot marbles with my American companions and hunted bare-handed for crabs and fish with Laotian families who visited from nearby farms. I was deputized by the women who arrived in the evening carrying baskets to collect cicadas that had singed their wings on the streetlights and dropped to the street. Each Buddhist New Year began with a days-long water balloon fight that seemingly the entire country took part in. Holidays took us every summer to a stretch of Malaysian coast where snake charmers competed for my attention with seaside ice-cream men. It was an existence that was the closest thing to Arcadia a child could know. There was a distant war in the mountains but it would be years before I knew what the words "Pathet Lao" and "Vietcong" meant.

After an abrupt exodus and my father's transfer to Saigon, my older brothers were sent to English boarding schools while my mother and I moved to Germany, her birth country. We lived in a village above the Rhine River chosen solely for its proximity to the forest. Our new home was at the foot of a mountain named after the biblical Mount of Olives, on whose flanks I seemed to spend endless afternoons, searching for mushrooms, evading Cheyenne and Lakota warriors, and hunting game with bow and arrow and a make-believe rifle, never killing anything but time. I attended a village school, learned German, and, by means of a newfound talent with a soccer ball, made friends in the schoolyard though I would always be known as "the American." I was never sure what being American required since I had only ever been to Florida on brief visits to a set of paternal grandparents. However, I accepted my title as an honorific since I was the only one to bear it.

After three years, I was told by my mother that we would be moving again, rejoining my father in a West African city which, I quickly discovered, was located only four degrees from the equator. This detail impressed me very much; I was at an age when the equator was a place of distinction. It was like being told that we would be living next door to the North Pole or in the vicinity of the Marianas Trench. I expected pitiless sunshine by day and intolerable steaminess at night, colossal insects below and oscillating primates above. To my dismay the climate turned out to be wholly bearable and rather than being in the bush, our new house was in an outlying district of ranch-style homes concealed by lush gardens and concrete walls and occupied mostly by French, Lebanese, and middle-class West Africans. The only wildlife I regularly encountered were a neighbor's pet antelopes, a bushbuck and a duiker, whose front legs had been purposefully broken and deformed as calves to slow any escape attempts and who came over periodically for their share of my breakfast cereal. After they were killed and eaten by local road builders, I took my revenge with bottle rockets fired at eye level.

I was a tireless reader in a way I never would be again and during the hottest hours of the day, I retreated to a wall in our yard shaded by pines and lost myself in L'Engle, London,

L'Amour, Grey, Steinbeck, Cornelius Ryan, and John Hersey as well as the Montgomery Ward Christmas catalog, which I examined and reexamined for much of the year, entranced by its skateboard and bicycle and Daisy rifle treasures. Thomas Berger's *Little Big Man* was my vade mecum for much of the seventh grade, read aloud one night by flashlight in tents pitched along the ocean to a multinational audience of fellow Scouts. I studied my father's whereabouts—he was forever traveling, it seemed—in a C. S. Hammond world atlas. Nouakchott, Niamey, N'Djamena, Ouagadougou, Lomé, Timbuktu, Dakar.

My nearest friends, two brothers from Bremen, lived a mile away and the shortcut to their home took me along a dirt path that descended into a shrubby valley. All the trees here had been cut down for firewood, leaving behind hillsides of red clay and patchy brushland, divided by a muddy gulch. A single wooden plank bridged the two sides.

Occasionally on my travels, I would be spotted and chased by a group of local boys. There was no reason for these pursuits other than the one imposed by custom everywhere: I was the outsider and they were the pack. I was a fast runner and vigilant enough never to have been caught, always reaching the safety of my destination in time. But one afternoon my luck ran out. I fled down the footpath with several silent boys not far behind. When I neared the trench, I realized that what on other days had been a routine sprint, my legs against theirs, had become an ambush. The plank, my bridge to safety, had been shoved aside and I was momentarily trapped. Turning, I pulled out the slingshot that I carried by habit, loaded it with a stone, and pointed it at my nearest pursuer, crying *"Arrête!"* By then, he was only steps away, a boy my age, ahead of the rest. I said that I would shoot if he came closer. We were like any two children, both unsure if this was still a game. Whether he took another step and whether I intentionally released my grip, I couldn't say for certain, but the stone hit him in the forehead point-blank. We stood stunned, by the blow, by the act. A tear slid down his cheek. "*Il faudra m'emmener avec vous à New York,*" he said. *You will have to take me with you to New York.*

I escaped that day, scrambling across the muddy channel to the far side of the ravine as the others arrived. In the remaining year that I spent there, I never again saw the boy who believed that all Americans lived somewhere called New York, but the core idea behind his words stayed lodged in my mind. New York was a place one wanted to reach.

Although my father was born and raised in East New York, he never talked about his childhood, its scarcities still a source of embarrassment rather than pride at how far he had come. The first real emissaries from New York that I met were two Harlem Globetrotters who were on a tour of West Africa with the team. (There wasn't a basketball court in the entire country so a swimming pool was drained and put into service.) I was worldly enough to know that New York wasn't a place entirely inhabited by dazzling giants, but also starry-eyed enough to begin to muse about a future lived not on the Western prairies that I so often read and daydreamed about but high above skyscraper canyons. And after a record called *Rapper's Delight* made its way across the Atlantic into my hands, the deal was more or less sealed.

It would take another decade before I made my way to New York with the misty ambition of becoming a writer. In the years between, I returned to Germany, where I was admitted to the realms of puberty and taverns at the same age, and then attended college in the Midwest. My first apartment wasn't an aerie above Manhattan, as I once imagined it would be, but instead, a ground-level arrangement on a quiet outer-borough street. A good word from a family friend landed me a job with literary lion George Plimpton of *The Paris Review*. In a strange coincidence, at about my age, my father, a top-of-his-class graduate of Yale Law School, had arrived for a job interview with Plimpton's father, the renowned attorney Francis Plimpton, only to be summarily dismissed for the blunder of showing up bareheaded. Happily, this Plimpton didn't stand on such ceremony. He would treat me with unexpected regard, giving more weight to my judgment than it deserved. And after I hit a game-winning home run at last light during a Central Park softball game against a crosstown rival, he looked at me with another kind of respect: the next time a former First Lady, twice-widowed and notoriously private, came over for pizza at the end of the workday, he invited me to stay for dinner.

The first bona fide writer that I met through my work with George Plimpton displayed a gun and offered me a drink when I arrived to deliver him his edited manuscript mid-morning; the second proposed oral pleasure. Another fooled around with my girlfriend (an occupational hazard in the literary field). I politely turned down the first two and threatened the third. Despite my bravado, I was reserved by temperament and I would sometimes think that I was in over my head in New York, an immigrant from the provinces. It was an impression that wouldn't entirely disappear for several years—at least until I met Sunny. He made one feel as though one had been waiting all one's life to arrive here.

After a year with Plimpton, I moved on to work at Columbia University as an aide-de-camp to a professor who was once the world's authority on Raymond Chandler but was now entering his senescence. I traveled an hour by subway twice a day, carried along as if by underground river (the 2 and 3 lines being stand-ins for Acheron and Styx, respectively), and from time to time, in the close quarters of our cars, I would look up from Philip Marlowe's troubles and notice a distant kinsman by the familiar afro-francophone accent or the tribal cheek scars once so common in that part of the world. I'd often think of my encounter by the ravine and of the two boys who wanted to come to New York. Only one of us made it here, so far as I knew and could ever know.

5

Two Rivers

"YOU DON'T GET A SECOND CHANCE TO MAKE A FIRST impression. And the impression I had of him was 'What an asshole.'"

I had just taken what was fast becoming my usual seat, a somewhat secluded spot in the deepest recess of the bar from which one could watch the entire room. Not far from me, Sunny was in conversation with two men, both named Richard. They belonged to a certain breed of homesteaders of which there were then no more than about a dozen in Red Hook—middle-aged painters and sculptors who had been drawn by the rock-bottom housing prices and the promise of a laid-back lifestyle. All seemed to be at the bar every Friday night.

"Who's an asshole?" I called out. In those early days it was often so quiet at Sunny's that one could both overhear and take part in every conversation that was occurring.

"Larry Rivers, Timmy."

Sunny was one of those men who added a "y" to names whenever he could. All Sals were Sally, Bobs were Bobby. I was Timmy. Larry Rivers didn't need it.

I looked at him blankly, the name not immediately registering.

"He's an artist," Sunny added, not condescendingly.

"Yes, I know who he is." I had actually once met the so-called grandfather of pop art in Plimpton's living room. "What did Larry Rivers ever do to cross you?"

In our brief friendship, I had already learned that Sunny not only had a passion for acting and theater (he kept a copy of his favorite play, John Guare's *The Loveliest Afternoon of the Year*, on a shelf behind the bar and during lulls he would sometimes put on his reading glasses and study the underlined passages), but that he also devoted much of his day to painting. Self-taught, he had taken it up in his twenties and from our conversations, I surmised that he had probably spent more time painting than he had engaged in any other single calling. He acknowledged he had never sold a painting, though—it seemed to be a matter of pride, as he was unwilling to put a price on his works. The closest he came was a bartering arrangement early in his career with the owner of an Upper East Side restaurant where he spent a year painting murals in exchange for French dinners. The restaurant and murals were still there. But one didn't have to go all the way uptown to see a Sunny Balzano. He had converted a storeroom in the rear of the bar into his studio and when I went to visit him there one afternoon, I saw large abstract paintings whose overlapping lines and dismembered figures were reminiscent of Willem de Kooning. His greatest influence, he told me that day, just ahead of Picasso and Cézanne. There was nothing amateurish about his art, but I had assumed that he had always worked in the same monkish isolation that he presently found himself in. I hadn't imagined him rubbing elbows with the likes of Larry Rivers.

"He must have been a real son of a bitch, Sunny," one of the Richards added. "You're usually as genial as the goddamn Dalai Lama."

I nodded my head in agreement. I had yet to hear Sunny be outright contemptuous of anyone. The one instance in which I saw him lose his patience, he addressed a self-appointed avant-gardist who was being a drunken nuisance with "Listen, you fuckin' banana," and the man looked equally stricken and dumbfounded.

"Well, it wasn't anything he did to me personally," he said, turning to include me. "What happened was, I was hired as a teaching assistant to Larry Rivers, who had been appointed to teach a summer workshop at Southampton College. It was the 1960s and a period in which I was quite involved in the downtown Manhattan art world and I was just beginning to make a name for myself."

One of the Richards must have given him a surprised look. "I don't want to make it sound like I'm blowing my own horn," Sunny quickly added. "Understand, I took my art very seriously for a time.

"Anyway," he continued, "Larry Rivers would come in once a week on his motorcycle, like he was James Dean—a middle-aged James Dean—and critique the students' work. But the reality of it was he didn't teach a damn thing. A lot of people enrolled in the class and mostly the students were dabblers and they were always going to remain that way, aye? And these poor students were there because they admired him, but whatever talent they had, Larry Rivers would destroy them. He was so shameful in his manner he would even cause people to cry."

A customer beckoned Sunny from down the bar and he excused himself. They exchanged a few words and Sunny reached into a drawer to sell the man a pack of black market Marlboros, but not before undoing the wrapper and slipping one out as his commission. Sunny smoked a great deal, being one of those people who considers a drink diminished without an accompanying cigarette and a story not properly told without one of each in hand.

"I'll never forget this older woman," he resumed after he returned, puffing on his commission. "Her husband had died, she had raised a family, and her kids were off on their own and she wanted to rededicate her life. Her paintings were simple, Grandma Moses–like. And Larry Rivers, he tells her, 'You're eighty years old, you've raised a family, you probably bake a great apple pie. Why don't you go home and bake pies?' "

He looked at each of us in turn, his expression deeply indignant.

"Isn't that *crass*? Isn't that *cruel*? Isn't that *terrible*?"

We all agreed that it was.

"What would it have taken for him to say, 'You know, you're doing very nice. Your space is this, your color is this, it has a charm, you've captured something really unique in the subject matter.' One could say a million things just to give her the feeling that what she was doing was worth continuing. After all, when you're eighty years old, you're not really doing this to make it in the art world. Like most people who paint, who play an instrument, who write, you do it because you love it. This is something she is going to do until the day she dies—if you treat her properly. But he put tears in her eyes and I wanted to get up there and belt the son of a bitch! Larry Rivers, he wasn't just an ordinary asshole. He was a *real* asshole, aye?"

Sunny excused himself again to attend to more business. One Richard looked at the other and turned his palms up. "I guess even saints have their enemies," he said. "The Dalai Lama's is China. Sunny's is fuckin' Larry Rivers."

As it neared ten o'clock, a brunette named Debbie, who bore a strong resemblance to Genevieve, the world-weary waitress in my favorite movie, *The Last Picture Show*, pulled a stool into the center of the bar and, guitar across her lap, began a cheerful dismantling of the human heart. There seemed to be only two kinds—the cheating and the broken. At the bar a few feet away, a Stetson-wearing customer named Fred made a show of turning his back to her. He was a singer as well, who usually accompanied himself with an electric guitar and a single foot-drum. Although there were others who would play intermittently from opening to last call, this was prime time at Sunny's, the hour when the bar generally began to fill, and these two feuded for this time slot with the intensity of late night talk show hosts. Both leaned as heavily on Jimmie Rodgers and Ernest Tubb as they did on Ray Price and Patsy Cline. There was often more than a little of *Red River* in Red Hook on Friday nights.

"Now, what can I get you, Timmy?" Sunny asked when he finally made his way back to my end of the bar. I had yet to be served but I felt no impatience. No one at Sunny's, on either side of the bar, was ever in a hurry.

Though usually a beer drinker of undiscriminating taste, impulsively I decided to ask for something different tonight. I ordered the first cocktail that came to mind. "You would like a Manhattan?" Sunny frowned. "Isn't that like going to Pittsburgh and ordering a Philly cheesesteak? We're in *Brooklyn,* Timmy."

"I hadn't thought of it that way. Well, what do you think I should have?"

"I'm only bustin' your balls. You know I'm not a real bartender by any stretch of the imagination and the truth of the matter is that I don't have the knowledge as how to make a Manhattan. But . . . why don't you have a berlermaker?"

"A berlermaker?"

"Yes. A pour of whiskey into a beer. It's what the men working longshore used to drink."

"A boilermaker?"

"That's what I said, Timmy. A berlermaker," Sunny said with a grin. "Let me get that for you."

As I watched Sunny make my boilermaker, pouring Four Roses whiskey into a collins glass and topping it off with Budweiser at a devastating ratio of one-to-one—a drink that would become "my drink" in the same way that I had begun to think of Sunny's as "my bar"—I thought to myself, not for the last time, that there was something timeless about him. He seemed to be a spirit sentenced to presiding over this bar for perpetuity. A kindlier version of Lloyd, eternity's bartender in *The Shining.*

I should have known better than to try and order a Manhattan. Sunny made conversation, not cocktails. He was, in fact, singularly inexpert at bartending. When one night someone asked whether they could have a martini, Sunny replied, "Yes, you may . . . but you're going to have to come around the bar and make it yourself!" So they did.

When he wasn't outright surrendering the bartending duties to customers, he was improvising as he went along. A wise guy's mistress once asked whether Sunny had any garnish for the Sex on the Beach she had ordered (God knows what he had put in it). "Certainly," he replied, without missing a beat and taking one of her bronzed hands into his. "Love is a smoke raised with the fume of sighs," he said. "Being purged, a fire sparkling in lovers' eyes. Being vexed, a sea nourished with lovers' tears." He paused and gave her a meaningful look. "What is it else? A madness most discreet," and handed her the glass. Somewhere, a maraschino cherry gave notice that night.

Sunny was staunchly impractical as a proprietor as well. Rather than install an ice machine, a bar fixture as essential as a Solomon Burke record, he emptied and refilled standard ice cube trays all week long until, by Friday, enough had accumulated to supply his one night of business. He kept the ice in a cooler below the bar, groping around with his hands when a drink required rocks. Although the digital age had arrived in America some years ago, Sunny continued to play beaten-up cassettes on a monophonic stereo. When Fred and Debbie weren't jockeying for the stage (the stage being whatever spot no one happened to be standing in) and there weren't fiddlers or accordionists communing in a booth, he would open a drawer and search through his modest selection: *The Songs of Audie Murphy*. Marilyn Monroe. Billie

Holiday. Julie London. Nat King Cole. Jimmy Durante, on whom Sunny must have modeled himself during his formative years. He usually put on his most prized recording, Chet Baker's *It Could Happen to You,* several times a night. No one seemed to mind.

SUNNY'S WAS AN easy place to come on one's own. The bar was a single long room (there was a back room where customers would go to make a call from a wooden phone booth but which was rarely in use otherwise). The oak bar took up the entire length of one side and three booths of sea-green Naugahyde benches most of the other. But there always seemed to be something to look at that one hadn't fully noticed before. For the art lover, there was the row of framed illustrations of semi-nude boudoir beauties by the late French boudoir-beauty specialist Maurice Milliere. Near the front door, one could examine the charcoal portrait of Sunny's great-grandfather and founder of the bar, Raffaele di Martini. Or a mussel-shell sculpture of unknown origin. For the lover of nautical themes, reproductions of sloops and brigantines battling high seas hung salon-style on the wall opposite the bar, while high above in the shadows, the U.S.S. *South Dakota* and other models of sailing ships sat in quiet repose, the dust in their miniature riggings a meditation on time itself.

There was also a full-size anchor, a guitar-like instrument made from a bedpan, a bust of JFK, a child's pair of coil-springed steel "Satellite Jumping Shoes" from the days of Sputnik and Laika, and a black-and-white photograph of several New York City harbor policemen standing on a patrol boat named the *Lieutenant Ronaghan.* There were doohickeys, thingamabobs, and whatsits. To the left of a bar mirror, a perfect set of shark's teeth gaped like a monster's misplaced dentures while to the right, a large button read, "Season's Greetings from the White House." A pair of ancient, cracked boxing gloves dangled from a nail and several homemade baseballs were arranged in a bowl like a boy's whimsical still life. Meanwhile, a single moldering leather shoe with a hole in its sole had a display shelf all to itself.

Midway between the two ends of the bar hung a copper wheelhouse bell. Occasionally a customer, not able to resist temptation, would strike the clapper, a near certain giveaway that he was new to the bar since he had just unwittingly announced that the next round was on him.

The task of lighting Sunny's was a collaborative effort on the part of a miscellany of fixtures. A couple of Pabst Blue Ribbon chandeliers and an electric Schaefer clock in the shape of a beer barrel were in charge of the bar, two Budweiser sconces the glassware shelves. The windowsill came under the jurisdiction of a pair of ship lanterns—one starboard green, the other port-side red—while responsibility for illuminating the room as a whole fell to the pale yellow bulbs fastened to the ceiling fans. The job of mood lighting was borne by several strings of colored Christmas lights and the odd hurricane lamp. In unison, they produced a gentle, exceedingly pleasant light, though some recesses of the bar were still so dark that if one had the urge to examine the back of one's hand, matches might need to be employed.

When one tired of looking at the wall art, there was always a diverting soul to draw one's attention. A private investigator and neighborhood activist named John sported a mustache that had not been trimmed since Abraham Beame was mayor and John was deputy city council president. When unspooled, it extended to his knees. A downhearted-looking truck driver named Tony with brilliant blue eyes, a fondness for western shirts, and, as I would learn in time, a life story sadder than a mill horse's (and the countenance to show for it) liked to stand in a corner with a guitar when no one was listening and sing songs such as "There Goes My Heart" and "Ballad of a Teenage Queen" with a delivery as unaffected by pitch as by any trace of happiness.

Another driver, this one of limousines, named Bobby had been inspired by Sunny to form a classical theater company several years earlier. He had named it the Brooklyn Stage Company and its earliest productions had been works by O'Neill, Beckett, and Shakespeare. Rehearsals had often taken place in the bar and each of the plays had had a short run at various makeshift stages in the neighborhood. But customers could be forgiven for thinking that the plays had never really ended. Bobby was a declaimer and there was a correlation between the amount of Irish whiskey he drank and the frequency and fervor of his declamations.

"I dreamed a dream tonight," he might suddenly announce to no one in particular.

"And so did I," would come the reply from a few heads down the bar.

"Well, what was yours?"

"That dreamers often lie," Sunny would shout.

"In bed asleep, while they do dream things true. Oh, then I see Queen Mab has been with you," Bobby would call out triumphantly and empty his glass. "Hit me with another one."

As I was coming to learn, when it came to Shakespeare,

Sunny could go toe-to-toe with anyone. Furthermore, he himself often sounded Shakespearean without intending to. One night a soprano would spontaneously sing "Mon Coeur S'ouvre à ta Voix" from the opera *Samson and Delilah,* and Sunny toasted the woman and her group of friends by saying, "I raise my glass to you. May it suffice to touch you all!"

The most fascinating object of study of all, of course, was Sunny himself. Sunny was so inextricably a part of the bar that if I didn't know better, I could have been easily convinced that both of them had come into being in the same instant, fully formed.

But as it turned out, Sunny was something of a recent returnee and the bar had only come to be known as "Sunny's" not long before I arrived. While the bar had been in his family its entire existence, Sunny's uncle John, along with Sunny's father, Ralph, had jointly run it for nearly all those years and by habit or tribute, some of the customers still referred to it as "John's." (If one looked closely, the trim of the awning above the door still read *John's Bar.*) The two brothers had never moved out of the neighborhood or indeed the house they were raised in, the tenement building adjoining the bar. At Red Hook's height of activity during World War II, the bar was one of a few dozen on the waterfront and only closed for a couple hours each day—between last call and breakfast. But when the wartime industry came to a halt and the ships began to leave and the neighborhood emptied out, John and Ralph watched the other bars close and the number of customers dwindle every year. The only adaptation they made to the changing times was to cut back the hours until by the mid-1980s they only opened during the day and only on weekdays, never making as much as a hundred dollars by nightfall.

Sunny, too, had joined the neighborhood flight, leaving days after high school graduation with no intention of ever living in Red Hook again. For thirty years, he followed callings that took him to SoHo and the Village, to California and as far as India, only paying his parents brief visits during that time. He didn't return home for good until he found himself in the darkened woods of middle age, off course and out of places to go and in need of family and familiarity. Penniless, he began helping his father and his uncle with the bar, taking over at midday for the few steadies who came in during the afternoon.

After Ralph's death in 1987, Sunny was left with the uneasy company of Uncle John, whom he tried hard not to antagonize. By constitution, Uncle John was intolerant of nearly everything and everyone and was universally opposed to change. When a retired police detective bought a brick warehouse across the street with plans to refurbish it in the hope of a neighborhood revival, John would stand on his stoop once a day, shake his fist and say, "That summabitch," and go back inside. He rarely drank and detested singing or reveling of any kind. His only expectation for the future was a series of drowsy days tapering off until he died, and the bar with him.

One Friday, Sunny asked whether he could stay open past sundown and after several "Why the fucks," he received his uncle's reluctant blessing. Sunny invited a neighbor who played the fiddle who, in turn, invited his musician friends. Uncle John, at several instances, rapped on the bar ceiling from the room above, but by the end of the night the bar had a few hundred dollars in the till. From then on, Uncle John gloomily agreed to let Sunny run the bar one night a week as he wished. After he died, Sunny closed the bar entirely. Except for Friday nights.

6

The Aleph

"I went along the wet street through one of the quietest and oldest quarters of the town. On the opposite side there stood in the darkness an old stone wall which I always noticed with pleasure. Old and serene . . . often during the day I let my eyes rest on its rough surface. . . . This time, too, the wall was peaceful and serene and yet something was altered in it. I was amazed to see a small and pretty doorway with a Gothic arch in the middle of the wall. . . . Probably I had seen it a hundred times and simply not noticed it. . . . Now that I looked more closely I saw over the portal a bright shield, on which, it seemed to me, there was something written. I strained my eyes and at last, in spite of the mud and puddles, went across, and there over the door I saw a stain showing up faintly on the grey-green of the wall, and over the stain bright letters dancing and then disappearing, returning and vanishing, once more. . . . Whoever hoped for any result from a display like that was not very smart. . . . Why have his letters playing on this old wall in the darkest alley of the Old Town on a wet night with not a soul passing by, and why were they so fleeting, so fitful and illegible? But wait, at last I succeeded in catching several words on end. They were:

MAGIC THEATER. ENTRANCE NOT FOR EVERYBODY."

—HERMANN HESSE, *Steppenwolf*

7

Balzanos and Travias

Sunny Balzano was born in August 1934, in a cold-water apartment next door to the bar, the same room his father had been delivered in twenty-six years earlier. He was the first child of his parents, Raffaele and Josephine, and the last to be delivered at home. His mother would give birth to six more children—Frank, Ralph, Rose, Joanne, Robert, and Louis. But it was to Sunny that she would always have the closest bond. She nursed him through the first year of his life as one day he would nurse her through the last year of hers.

The first sounds of the world beyond the windows that he would have heard would have been the lunch whistle letting loose hundreds of dockworkers, their shouts as they rushed into the Balzano family bar next door, the bleating of foghorns from the harbor, the backfiring of trucks, the cutting of steel by welders at the iron works across the street. And among the first smells he may have smelled were those of paint and shellac and turpentine from Miles Paints, the small manufacturer next door where his father and grandfather worked intermittently. In a few years, Miles Paints would close and the Animal Hair Manufacturing Company, a company that processed horse, cow, and boar hair for brushes and brooms and violin bows, would move in and periodically a slaughterhouse truck would dump ears and tails and manes in piles behind the building. In the summer, the flies and stench of decaying flesh would seep into the Balzanos' rooms despite the shut windows and Sunny would think back fondly on the fumes of shellac and turpentine the way others remember the fragrance of apple blossoms wafting in the bedroom window of their childhood home at night.

Sunny had been delivered by the midwife to a front row seat on one of the busiest deep-sea ports in the country, a crossroads of shipping and rail and truck. His family home was midway between two ship basins, the Atlantic and Erie, which, upon their completion in the mid-1800s, had made Red Hook the gateway to the Erie Canal. The sugar, the coffee, the tropical produce destined for Cleveland, Chicago, and beyond, came through its port. There was noise all the time. Today it would be like living next to the tarmac of Kennedy Airport.

By the time of Sunny's birth, the Balzanos had already resided in this corner of Red Hook for more than a quarter century. His grandfather Antonio had arrived from Calabria in 1888 as a fourteen-year-old, his grandmother Angelina di Martini in 1896 as a twenty-year-old. The two married in 1898 and shared a tenement with her parents, Raffaele and Maria Grazia, at the northern end of Red Hook until 1907, when Antonio bought Sunny's birth house, a three-story redbrick building at 251 Conover Street, for $1500, and the entire family, including grandparents, moved to the Point.

Although they now lived directly down the street from the piers, and shipyards were by far the largest employers in Red Hook, Antonio was unlikely to have been chosen during the shape-ups, then dominated by Irish hiring bosses. He was a slight man who spoke little English. For a time, he worked in a hat store before starting up with Miles Paints. For thirteen years he saved until he had enough money to buy the building next door at 253 Conover, intending to open a bar in its street-level storefront with his father-in-law. The year was 1920, the same year that Prohibition began. This may seem as providential as going into the typewriter ribbon business in 1990. But in a community like Red Hook, a law against liquor consumption would have been as enforceable as a ban on nocturnal erections. It's only a mild overstatement to say that nearly every adult male who lived in this quarter of Red Hook was what today would be considered an alcoholic. With the same low regard for the well-being of others as the crack dealers of later times, some Red Hookers during this time sold "smoke"—denatured alcohol cut with milk—from their storefronts and restaurants. In 1922, one such batch sold on Conover Street killed twelve and blinded six. Ten years later smoke was still being made and when a reporter asked a resident of a Red Hook shantytown known as Tin Can City what kind of person would buy the stuff, he was told, "Only dumb fellers drink poison. Then they die. There's no trouble, and if the police don't come around, we bury them and the thing is closed."

Antonio never sold smoke. The Volstead Act allowed

each household to produce two hundred gallons of home-made wine a year. If one owned two adjoining houses, had a well-concealed backyard, and a stream of workers passed by your front door all day and much of the night, it was not hard to see the entrepreneurial possibilities of this loophole. So for the first dozen years of its existence, Balzano's didn't serve beers and shots—the usual staples of a laborers' bar—but wine fermented in four fifty-gallon barrels in the basement. After one of Antonio's daughters married a Southerner named Hoppes and the two moved into the building, Antonio took advantage of his son-in-law's native expertise, supplementing the bar income by discreetly distilling whiskey in one of the upstairs apartments. The product was good enough for export—to Staten Island and New Jersey. By this time, Antonio's sons Raffaele (Sunny's father, now known as Ralph) and John had joined the family concern and father and sons took care of delivery themselves, by suitcase.

Ralph Balzano first saw his future wife, Josephine, in one of the many Coney Island wine gardens that operated openly during Prohibition. This one happened to belong to his aunt Mary and her husband, Dominick. Josephine was half an orphan. When she was an infant, her mother had leaned against the kitchen stove to keep warm and her cotton petticoat caught on fire, the sudden blaze consuming her. Her father, Francisco Travia, had taken her and her younger brother Anthony to a charity ward run by Irish nuns. The orphanage was something out of Dickens transplanted to Brooklyn's southern shoreline. There were privations and beatings and humiliations. When she was a teenager, Francisco came one day and took her to live with his brother Dominick and his wife, Mary. But there her sense of captivity only heightened.

She was put to work in the wine garden, where she cleaned the toilets, chopped firewood, and served men who leered at her and pinched her when she walked by with her hands full. She pushed a cart of roasted chestnuts on the newly built Coney Island boardwalk until one morning she bent to light the stove beneath the cart and the kerosene vapors exploded in her face. Fire seemed to be a curse that ran in her family. Her aunt bathed her skin with lemon juice and iodine for weeks. She took Josephine to some industrial vats in the neighborhood that emitted gaseous fumes, and, in the belief that inhaling these was somehow medicinal, the two would stand next to the vents and breathe deeply. Even years later, after she had moved away from Coney Island and had had children of her own, Josephine would periodically make the pilgrimage back to inhale the gases with her aunt. People came from all over the borough to that spot. It was the Lourdes of Brooklyn.

Coney Island was known as "the people's playground" but when Josephine tried to do anything playful herself, like wearing makeup or going on a date, her uncle would search the Steeplechase Park, the rides, the seats of Loew's Kings Theatre, and if he found her, he would kick her all the way home.

When Ralph saw all this, he came home one night and told his parents that they needed to rescue this distant relative by marriage from a life of mistreatment by bringing her to live with them in Red Hook. His motives were both altruistic and logistic. It was a way to liberate her from Uncle Dominick's tyranny but also to bring her physically closer to him. His parents agreed and before long, Ralph and Josephine were married, in 1933 at Red Hook's Church of the

Visitation. By Christmas, Josephine was pregnant with Sunny.

Sunny's extended family were unusual, and sometimes mysterious, people. The most educated of his relatives was his uncle Louis Anatriello who, before marrying one of his aunts, had gone to whistling school in Italy and whose Sunday visits were announced by the chirrups and trills of warblers and wagtails and thrushes. His grandparents Balzano, who lived upstairs, never called each other by their real names, Antonio and Angelina, but rather Marc Antone and Juliet, as if they had wandered away from two different Shakespeare plays and run off together to start new lives in Brooklyn. His grandmother towered over her husband in height and girth, though her weight was largely distributed to her bosom. She was known in Red Hook as a *maga,* a woman who could summon the power of the saints, cast and undo spells, heal the ailing, and change the fortunes of the unlucky. In a neighborhood where people filled their homes with plaster statuaries of saints, the understudies of the Roman and Greek gods petitioned by their ancestors, Angelina bartered her talent for chickens, bananas, coffee. Her superstitions were those of Southern Italians—part Catholic, part idiopathic. She feared the evil eye, *il malocchio,* and frequently warded it off by pointing the sign of the devil's horns at the ground. She believed there were hidden patterns in numbers, a trait that she passed down to her eldest grandson. Half a century later he still searched the tallies on receipts and the serial numbers on dollar bills for clues as to how to play the lotto. Angelina confessed to the priest and prayed to Mary and thought of Christ several times a day, and yet when she made a protective charm for Ralph to carry on his person, a pouch wrapped in cloth, it contained rosary beads but also a Buddha. How a statuette of Siddhartha came into her possession and what she believed it to invoke are a mystery lost to time.

Sunny's maternal grandfather, Francisco Travia, who had left his daughter at the orphanage, was even slighter than Antonio and lived in Coney Island, where he worked at the Blowhole Theater in Steeplechase Park as a cowboy clown. He never remarried after his wife succumbed to fire, and when he got out of work in the evenings, rather than return to his empty room he preferred to search the boardwalk and the sand for pieces of jewelry, little trinkets, combs with missing teeth, toy shovels, and discarded Steeplechase tickets that hadn't been entirely punched. He would make little packages for his grandchildren for when he came up to Red Hook. In the spring, he would bring them chicks or baby rabbits. He spoke broken English and even as a young child Sunny sensed that his grandfather was a kind of stranger in the world, a tormented man who only really seemed at peace when he held his grandson on his lap and murmured softly in Italian to him. In truth, he had briefly been an infamous figure in New York, accused of a grisly crime, but this was a family secret so closely held that Sunny wouldn't come to fully know it until he himself was an old man.

8

The Japanese Zero
That Sank in the
Mississippi-Hudson River

LATE IN THE SPRING AND LATE IN THE EVENING, WE placed our jackets over our stools and headed for the door. "Sunny, we'll be back in a bit."

"You fellows, you be careful," Sunny replied gravely.

Outside, across the street, a green-lit tugboat returning from the fuel pumps in Erie Basin glided by and across the water the shore lights of Staten Island smoldered. Bell buoys dinged in the dark as if clanging for an underwater fire.

There were three of us: Jimmy, Jon, and myself. They were among the few friends I had begun to bring along to Red Hook, knowing they would appreciate Sunny and his magnificent bar. We shared that certain recklessness particular to bachelors. In our late twenties, we still had parents but no wives or children to feel a responsibility toward. We had begun swimming in the harbor weeks earlier and by now had a kind of routine. We never swam before midnight. This was not a rule; we just needed time to drink. Sobriety has its virtues but impulsiveness isn't one of them, and foolhardy impulse is surely at the root of most adventures. So, we would have boilermakers (my friends had been easily persuaded that this was the only fitting drink at Sunny's) and either talk amongst ourselves or try to get Sunny's attention in the hope he would tell us a story.

Eventually one of us would get the restless itch and he'd motion to the other two and we would slip off our stools. I'd usually call out to Sunny to let him know where we were going and he'd invariably respond with a worried frown, his quiet way of saying, "Timmy, do me a kindness. Don't fuck with the water."

Sunny knew the harbor. Or rather, he knew that no one can ever know the harbor. The water speeds up as it crosses shallows over what perhaps once had been breakwaters, and slows abruptly over pools tucked into the shoreline. It curls into itself, creating swirling vortexes that disappear and reappear with the tides. Waves materialize unexpectedly from the wake of the far-off Staten Island Ferry. Sunny knew that water could turn on you. He and I would both be reminded of it one day, but that is another story.

On that spring night, my friends and I crossed the street and walked the two blocks to the nearest jetty. We hushed as we passed the night watchman near the brick warehouse sleeping in his shack lit by a blue television glow. On the backside of the building, the wooden pier jutted out at the elbow of Red Hook so that the Statue of Liberty lay straight ahead across the open harbor, Governors Island and lower Manhattan were off to the right beyond a narrow stretch of water called Buttermilk Channel, and the Verrazano-Narrows Bridge twinkled to our left. A Swiss woman I once knew had exclaimed while driving by the Verrazano, "Bridges are like cathedrals to me!" She was excited about America and disposed to saying things like *"J'aime graffiti!"* but looking southward at that string of pearls from this pier, I knew what she meant.

We stripped and started crab-walking across the oily rocks that led down to the water. Tiny barnacles eked out a living here; on mornings after these swims I'd often wake in bed and not immediately remember the night before until I'd look down at my feet and see the cuts they'd made.

Once we had come this far, there was no turning back. The tide could be running fearsomely strong, but with our feet scraped and greasy and briny, we'd sooner take our chances with the current than crawl back up the mucky rocks and have nothing to show for the night but the smell of ocean funk. The darkness concealed most drifting debris and if one of us spotted a familiar limp latex shape floating by, which we did with some regularity, there always had to follow a crack about the Coney Island Whitefish running that night. The Gowanus Herring. The Red Hook Shad.

We lined up, balancing unsteadily on the rocks, taking in this panorama of ours, trying to overcome the last doubt that always came at this moment. Suddenly a harbor patrol boat appeared around the jetty, not more than two hundred yards from shore. We stood as still as marble replicas of ourselves, unsure whether it was legal or not to be standing naked on the edge of New York Harbor in the middle of the night. Jim, a psychologist by day who perhaps was now giving momentary thought to his practitioner's license, muttered softly, "Nothing happening here, officer." If anyone on board spotted us they didn't let on; the boat continued its steady path up the channel like the refined society lady who is unruffled by lewd illustrations defacing a Park Avenue wall as she strides past. Soon we were left in the quiet once more, with the wake lapping against the rocks at our feet.

Some nights the water would rush northward in a continual surge and only being a strong swimmer had kept me abreast of the rocks. I would have visions of myself clawing my way ashore in Manhattan, pale and apparitional like a revenant, and startling some lovers sitting on a waterside bench.

Impulsive harbor swimmers don't consult tidal charts, but that night we arrived at slack tide and the water was as still as it ever would be here. I crouched close to the water's edge, as you had to make a shallow dive. One could never be certain what the terrain was like beneath the water. More than once, I had gotten my feet tangled in twisted steel rebar while trying to climb out. When I hit the water, still cold in June, my body rang, the inner alarm bells all sounding at once, and I took ten, fifteen strokes before coming up for breath. My friends were just behind me. We easily swam out several hundred feet before rolling over onto our backs. Warehouses stood in silhouette behind us. In that dark shoreline there was a speck of orange light as insignificantly small as a single glowworm on the far side of a meadow, but unmistakably coming from the bar, and it seemed inexpressibly strange that minutes ago we had been contained in that speck.

I have looked at the city from the 102nd floor of the Empire State Building, from planes banking over the Hudson, from Central Park West penthouses. I would one night walk the suspension cables to the top of the Brooklyn Bridge, risking tabloid headlines, Rikers Island, and, of course, death, to have an unobstructed panoramic view. But I would never feel more a part of New York than when I was drifting in its harbor and looking at its lights—the shore lights, the skyscraper lights, the bridge lights, the ferry lights, the moonlight above, the phosphorous lights below, and us out in the middle of it all, bobbing corpuscles in the city's bloodstream.

Why did we do this? Perhaps it was the old saw that one goes out into the wilderness—and for us, the harbor was wilderness—to be off the map of one's daily life, to a place where one is nobody, one is nowhere, and where one has the feeling of being most alive.

We didn't say any of this, of course. Instead we whooped in the chilly water and Jon shouted, "This is better than cocaine." I wasn't so sure he had ever taken cocaine, but I understood. The harbor swimming rush was powerful and, as borne out by the many nights we would return to this spot, addicting. We never stayed in long, aware of hubris's downside and knowing that our drinks were waiting and Sunny was nervously watching the door.

On that night and others, we swam ashore and pulled on our clothes and walked back the way we had come, past the dreaming night watchman and to the three barstools with our jackets draped over them. Perhaps this, as much as any other reason, was why we were harbor swimmers—the feeling of returning to the security of the bar, knowing that while the drinking and smoking and flirting and talking had continued uninterrupted in this room, we had, for a few moments, not only stepped outside but into another world.

SUNNY SAW US come back in with our hair and clothes still a little wet, our moods giddy, and he wandered over and said, "You guys didn't happen to see my ring out there?"

"Your ring, Sunny? What's that?"

"My Zero ring. It's been there for, oh, over fifty years now."

Although we had only known him for a short time, we already knew of Sunny that he had once commandeered a B-29 bomber down a runway in the dead of night, been discovered in flagrante by both the Bell Telephone man and Andy Warhol (the telephone man apologized profusely and Warhol asked whether he could go get his film camera), dispatched a rabble of rats that had invaded his house with a .22 rifle, and ridden polo horses with the staff of the municipal waterworks in a place called Mount Abu in the Indian state of Rajasthan. Sunny told elaborate discursive histories of his past, of the past in general, and loved to eulogize his forebears, our forebears (that is, those who had sat on these same barstools), and his younger self. We'd prompt him some nights by saying, "Sunny, was Hitler's yacht really moored over on Coffey Street?" or "What would Hubert Selby drink when he hung out here?" There was something scripted about these moments, as if Sunny was just waiting for his cue. We were happy to say our lines.

"Zero ring? What are you talking about, Sunny?"

"Oh, I haven't told you about my Zero ring? That's strange. Let me see now," he began, tapping his ever-present cigarette. "Well, it was one of the very early traumas that I had in my life. I had an uncle. Uncle Tony. He was my mother's only brother and she loved him dearly. So did I. He was very quiet and he left a lot to the imagination so that one had to fill in the gaps—and that with which a child fills those gaps is always more magnificent than the truth, aye? Well, he was drafted into the army during the war. I must have been about nine or ten. Uncle Tony ended up in Guam, which was the base for many of the operations in the Pacific. It was susceptible to Japanese bombings and we were very fearful as to what might happen to Uncle Tony. I remember how the *Daily News* would give accounts of dogfights and of how many American planes had been shot down. So we were always very aware of the war and the importance of Guam to what was taking place.

"Well, Uncle Tony was a machine gunner. What exactly that meant I wasn't sure, but when we used to play war, I was always my uncle Tony. I would find exhaust pipes that fell off cars and trucks—in those days, you hit any kind of bump, half the car would fall off. So I would find exhaust pipes and I would pretend they were machine guns.

"Uncle Tony used to write what were called victory letters. Well, I couldn't read these victory letters because, to tell the truth, I couldn't read at all. You see, I was dyslexic and back then they didn't know about these things so they regarded you as being somewhat stupid. It hurts me even now when I think about it. I went to Catholic school and when I considered the nuns who I thought were supposed to be instilled with qualities of understanding and mercy and love,

I'd like to think that they would have at least been able to extend themselves to a greater degree than they did. They tended to help those children who were very adept, who were smarter, rather than those of us who had some kind of handicap. They gave assistance more to those that had it, not to those who needed it. That didn't make any sense. In hindsight, I think, 'My goodness, how could an individual who was so educated have been so stupid and insensitive as to not know that you don't help those who have it, you help those that need it?' And God knows, I needed their help and I didn't get it."

Sunny paused and looked down the bar, his expression suddenly pained. The remaining customers were clustered in the corner, talking amongst themselves. He lit a new cigarette. Sunny's way of storytelling could be so digressive that both he and listener often forgot the topic.

"Sunny, go on about Uncle Tony," someone said.

"Forgive me for going off like that, but that's my way. So, I couldn't read but my mother would read the victory letters to us and to what degree that he could, Uncle Tony would say how he was. The way mail was sent, all communications had to go through some authority. That speaks to the secrecy that was considered necessary to fight a war. The letters were short but what they really validated was, 'He is alive.' Or at least he was alive when he wrote to us.

"Anyway, at some pernt, we received a victory letter and inside the letter was an aluminum ring and my Uncle Tony wrote: 'This ring was made from a Japanese Zero that I shot down and I am sending it as a gift to Sunny.'

"Wow. A Japanese Zero! I was so proud. I put that ring on my ten-year-old finger. My pinky, actually. That gives you an idea of the size of the ring. I leave the house and I'm going to brag to all my friends. I was so full of enthusiasm. I ran to the White Rock pier over by Van Dyke Street. Half the neighborhood seemed to work there and we never had to buy a soda in all of our childhood lives. We'd go to the plant and peek in and they'd give us a case and we'd hang the bottles from ropes in the water to keep them cool. Like that.

"Anyway, we all hung out by the pier. It had to be around the beginning of summer. The *Brooklyn Eagle* would come by every year and give each of us a dime to dive naked from the piers into the river. They'd photograph us and they would use that to announce the beginning of summer. We always swam naked. No girls were allowed. There weren't any press people taking pictures there that day but it was about that time of year.

"So I knew everyone would be at the pier and I ran down there to do as kids do—to brag to my friends that my uncle shot down this Zero. We were all so conscious of the war. If you were a four-year-old kid you knew there was a war, some place where your father or your uncle or a relative was fighting. It was such an effort by the whole of America, or at least the America I knew, which was this little corner of Red Hook. We never threw a can away. They'd collect in piles on the street and we knew that those piles would be taken away to build tanks out of. So, I ran to the docks and I shouted, 'Guys, look what I got!'

" 'What the fu-uck is that?' someone called out.

" 'A ring,' I said. 'My uncle Tony shot down a Japanese Zero and he made me this ring out of it.'

"There was one guy and I'm gonna say his name. I don't like to say names when I tell stories but if he's alive and he ever hears this story from anyone, I want him to know that he broke my heart. Richie Ross. I'll never forget him. These guys, some of them were a bunch of bananas, and Richie Ross—he was one of the bullies of the crowd. I don't know how old he was but he seemed to be a giant to me. He and his cousin, Goofy Gilbride, they were always bullying and once I stabbed Goofy Gilbride in the leg when he went too far with his teasing. He had to have been young and soft because the blade was so dull and it would have just bent ordinarily but it went in deep. Should have cut him in the balls, actually.

"Well, Richie Ross said, 'Let me see that Japanese Zero ring.'

"I can't say I gave it to him. I took it off my pinky and I held it up and he snatched it out of my hand. And then he proceeded to stick it on his little penis. I remember how he pulled his skin—we weren't circumcised in those days—and he managed to get it on! He really stuck it back there and I cried, 'Give me my Zero ring!'

" 'I got your fuckin' Japanese Zero ring. You want it, you come and take it!'

"He was sort of dancing around in circles and shaking his little dicky. I said, 'Come on, Richie. Give me my ring. My uncle shot down a Japanese Zero and made me that ring and I want it. Please, Richie.'

" 'I got it. You want it. You come and take it.'

"I said, 'I'm not going to take it. Give me my fuckin' ring!'

"Meantime, his little dicky started to get hard. Here's this little ring stuck on his little prick and it's choking him, you see? And he's trying to get it off now, and he can't get it off because the more he tries, the harder he gets.

"At that pernt, he was almost crying from the pain of it. So he jumps into the cold water figuring that's going to make his prick go down and he'll get the ring off. And the ring does get loose and it comes off and it sinks to the bottom of the Mississippi-Hudson River.

"I'm laughing now as I'm telling you this, but I cried. I cried. I got home and my mother—she was so proud of my uncle and she said, 'Sunny, where's your ring?' and I told her I was down at the docks and it came off my finger in the water and it sank. I couldn't tell the truth. How was I going to tell the truth? How could I? That day, I hated the fucking Japanese, but I hated Richie Ross more!"

The bar was quiet. Pinky Tomlin had stopped crooning on the radio long ago and Sunny smoked and we sipped our bottles. "Sunny, that's a beautiful story beautifully told," I finally said. "But ... why do you call it the Mississippi-Hudson River?"

"Timmy, those docks. I think about them now and I realize folks won't really understand if I just call it the Hudson River. Calling it the Mississippi-Hudson conveys the idea that we all had a little of Tom Sawyer and Huck Finn in us— though we had more fun there than those two ever had. We had everything. Everything came here, everything went from here, and the adventures we would have, they weren't make-believe like Huck Finn and Tom Sawyer. They were real.

"The cops used to come with their billy clubs and we would run under the pier and they would yell, 'Come out, you little shits!' and we'd yell, 'Brass button, blue coat, can't catch a fuckin' nanny goat!'

"We never meant harm by it. We were basically good. But we did some bad shit. The ships would sometimes send a launch boat to shore and tie it up to a dock and the men would go to buy supplies. We'd steal the boat and then let it go so it'd drift away. You think of the sailors who came here from all around the world and when they got here, this is what they thought New York was. But this wasn't New York. It was Red Hook. The people who were born and raised down here, we were different. Those people who lived in other neighborhoods, across Hamilton Avenue or even here in the projects, they graduated high school. Some went to college. We were like urchins down here. We grew up in a culture that was unique to Red Hook. We didn't know anything about what those people knew and we didn't know why we didn't like them but we didn't like them. We had this thing we used to say, 'We're the boys from Red Hook you hear so much about/ Every time we go down the street you hear the people shout/ Here come the boys from Red Hook you hear so much about!' We loved being talked about that way. We took pride in being bad because it was our notoriety. We weren't acclaimed for being good. Or for being educated. We were notorious. That's the way it was. We tended to be badder than most. And those who weren't as bad as most, pretended to be bad as most.

"But I wasn't bad in the sense that I wanted to hurt anybody. If you hurt somebody, you hurt yourself more. You know what I mean, Timmy. Jon. Jimmy. I could tell you a lot of stories that took place on those docks, and I'm sorry for some of the things we did because those poor guys didn't deserve it. You realize when you start talking about these things that when you're young you try to hide a lot of the shit you did from yourself. You don't allow yourself to realize the full impact of what you've done. But when you begin to talk

about it thirty, forty, fifty years later, like we're doing right now, you remember the things you'd think you'd forget. You don't forget. In fact, the older you get, the more you remember the stuff with a clarity that you could never conceive you would have. You remember with regret, but what you also remember is the poetry of it. I mean, all these things that have taken place, it's what you are. You are everything you've ever done. So, after all these years, you throw a lot of the bullshit, a lot of the excuses away. I was never malicious. I wasn't the kind who ever set out with a mind to hurt anyone. Not like Richie Ross and Goofy Gilbride.

"In a way, remembering this as I am tonight, I'm reliving it again, in a different way. You need the time between the experience and the time of remembrance. It's like wine that needs to ferment. Wine has to have the time in order to give birth to something really beautiful. And experience is the same way. It takes a lot of time to go from life to art, but if you wait long enough, it'll give birth to poetry. It has to be that way. I really enjoy remembering in the way I do. I wouldn't want to remember what I did yesterday because it hasn't fermented properly. It'd be cheap wine!"

Sunny belonged to a vanishing breed of barstool rhetorician, which in him seemed to have reached its apotheosis. He strung words together not only into a few memorable sentences but into long luminous paragraphs, the beginning, the middle, and the end of his tales already perfectly formed. He did this effortlessly and without prior rehearsal, his mind seemingly sharpened rather than dimmed by liquor.

"Anyway, that was the story of the Japanese Zero. It was shot down in Guam and sunk in the Mississippi-Hudson River."

9

Young Virginia Woolf

Sunny's was an immensely romantic place, but ac-tual romance was hard to come by. The ratio of men to women at the bar in those days was Alaskan. When a new woman did walk through that door on a Friday, it was as startling as spotting a bird in flight while midway across the ocean. You were filled with the same wonder—that this crea-ture had arrived *here;* the same curiosity—at what motivated her to wander so far from whatever world she was usually at home in; and above all, you were usually filled with the same hope—that this being would come over and perch next to you and keep you company as you sailed on through the night.

This occurred very seldom. Sunny's was far off most mi-gratory paths.

Overtly making advances toward a woman was not pro-hibited by Sunny. This was still a bar and we were still men. But behaving honorably was paramount. I rarely saw Sunny intercede to deliver a woman from unwanted advances because it was understood that being disrespectful to any person here was being disrespectful to Sunny and to most of the men, being put out of his bar would be as crushing an expulsion as any from life's feast. So a kind of old-fashioned decorousness dictated the men's behavior—no doubt in part because many of the men were older (I overheard one septuagenarian socialist say to a young off-duty waitress one night after she had affectionately squeezed his arm, "Do you think it might be possible for you and I to make sweet love all night long?"), but also because the laws of attraction and alcohol and rash concupiscence that usually misgovern our actions seemed to be in suspension here. Or as Sunny would put it, "At my bar, people are able to be more than what they are, not less than what they are, as is typically the case in bars."

My own amatory experiences at Sunny's were limited not just by the scarcity of women but by my relative greenness in matters of love. The only encounter that came to any fruition occurred after I had been asked by a voluptuous brunette, who to my surprise had been eyeing me with unmistakable erotic contemplation, whether I'd come for a walk down to the pier to look at the water. The culmination of the experience—some kissing with beer on our breaths and brine in the air—was less the consummation of ardor than a sense of actually being consumed. She was the robust type.

More typical of my fumbling attempts to meet someone was the night I saw the Red Baron. I arrived one Friday evening, sat on a barstool, ordered a drink from Sunny, and, looking down the bar, saw at the far corner a strikingly beautiful woman. She was tall, wore her long hair simply, and had wrapped a red scarf around her neck. I immediately named her the Red Baron (though when a friend asked me to describe her the following day, I said she resembled "a young Virginia Woolf"—surely the first time the two historical figures have been conflated). I resolved to meet her after a few more sips, but when I turned to look again in her direction, she was putting on her coat and preparing to leave.

I leaned across the bar and said, "Sunny, please. Do you have something I can write on?"

Sunny had followed my gaze and guessed my intent.

"Not for nothing, Timmy," he said as he handed me pen and paper, "but one never wants to be so blatant as to put one's head in the guillotine."

"Huh?"

"Let me put it this way. Although I am a great flirt, I am not and have never been an overt one. I always do it within the framework of respect and I always leave a question as to whether—'Is he or is he not flirting?'—so I got a way out, aye?"

I still consider this some of the soundest advice I have ever had on the matter.

Instead of my phone number, I quickly wrote down the names of two books by Bohumil Hrabal, the great Czech writer known for customarily receiving his visitors while seated at a table in an ancient Prague tavern that I imagined was not entirely unlike Sunny's. This was a time when I believed that knowing a person's favorite books said more about them than anything they could say in passing during a few moments in a bar, and so I was going to let an old Czech do the talking for me. As she passed behind me I swiveled on the barstool and said, "You dropped this," and handed her the folded piece of paper. She took it from me and, with a puzzled look, continued to the door. I thought to myself as I turned back to my beer, *It's all right, Tim. We're all stumbling through life.*

The Red Baron never returned. I like to think that circumstances intervened. That she was getting married or that she had left on an around-the-world trip the next day, perhaps picking up a couple of novels while passing through Brno or Ostrava.

Over the years, as more women and younger customers began to come to Sunny's, I would observe other notes being passed. Later, I would become the courier, and occasionally the recipient, of some of these letters. Some were left beneath tips and some were sent via the actual U.S. Postal Service. One was a dispatch written on a coaster at another bar and sent as a postcard. The most unusual communication I would receive was a large manila envelope sent by a young woman from Minneapolis I had met only once. It contained a college term paper she had written on the overlooked role that Minnesotans played in the Spanish-American War—she asked what advice I might have in turning it into a musical.

There is one note that I still carry with me to this day, one that I consider as romantic a gesture as has ever been made to me by a stranger.

On a rare busy night, I was helping Sunny ferry beers, as I had begun to do. There were two women seated close to the middle of the bar and engrossed in conversation. They must have tried and failed to get my attention—the next time I hurried by, one of them had left a note flat on the bar, a request for drinks and more Goldfish crackers. As I returned with their order, I looked at them more closely. There was something of a cowgirl about the one on the left with her checked shirt, her blue jeans, and hair that actually was the color of late-summer prairie. We spoke for several minutes, during which she told me she had come to the city from Oklahoma and that she built theater sets, and I told her how I had once written a note at this bar and how I had passed it to a woman who had reminded me of a young Virginia Woolf. I was called away and as I looked back a minute later I saw that she was writing again. Other customers kept me busy and as she was getting ready to leave later that night, she came to where I was standing and silently handed me a slip of paper and turned and walked out. On one side she had written "Marisa" and on the other she had written from memory:

> Mr. Ramsay, stumbling along a passage one dark morning, stretched his arms out, but Mrs. Ramsay having died rather suddenly the night before, his arms, though stretched out, remained empty.
>
> —*To the Lighthouse*, V. WOOLF

10

Speakeasy

SUNNY WAS A MAN OF PARTICULARLY EASY VIRTUE. Though in many ways he had the habits and tastes of an old man, he had some of the appetites of a teenager in his lusty prime. He loved to be in love and his often-bawdy anecdotes suggested a lifelong love life of passing entanglements, the abundance of which would have put Errol Flynn to shame at his own comparative carnal inadequacy. Sunny was a bachelor's bachelor, a role model to those customers who daydreamed about a less domesticated existence than the ones they found themselves in. So when he announced that he had met a woman with whom he had fallen in love, a Norwegian artist several decades younger than he, and that he had asked her to move in with him, there were considerable murmurs of surprise, some expressions of doubt, and one or two outright cries of dismay, as if the last partisan had raised the white flag. But the artist soon began appearing alongside him on Fridays. With Nordic features and a tomboy haircut, she was an attractive but conspicuously shy woman; her shoulders were usually hunched forward like the child who is ever trying to go unnoticed. Her name was spelled Tone though she pronounced it "Tuna." "Like the fish," she would say.

It wasn't only their disparity in age that made them an unlikely match. Tone was as reserved as Sunny was demonstrative. She came from an island in the North Sea and a religious upbringing so cloistered that although she had gone to art school on the mainland, she seemed at times still to be acclimating herself to the tastes of the modern world. She was often unfamiliar with pop culture references and uncomfortable with practices that others might take for granted—she confided to me in an early conversation that she neither danced nor went to the beach. The idea of being in public in a mere swimsuit mortified her. Meanwhile, Sunny had the air of the unabashed nudist about him.

Tone spoke English fairly well and was already freely using local expressions such as "I don't know from nothing" and "Fuhgeddaboudit," the latter albeit with a Norse cadence that re-separated the phrase into distinct words. But her understanding of certain American expressions, including standard drink orders, was still developing and when I would ask for a boilermaker, which in Sunny's rendition had always meant a shot of whiskey poured into a glass of beer, she would look at me uncertainly and ask, "You mean a submarine?" I had never heard of a drink called a submarine and decided she had to be thinking of the depth charge, the showy and teeth-imperiling variation on the boilermaker in which a shot glass is actually dropped into the beer.

"Sure. A submarine," I would say, and she would happily bring me the usual boilermaker.

Tone did not always come in on Fridays and when she did she rarely had the stamina to stay till sunrise, which was often the time that Sunny bid his last customer good night. Sunny's own stamina would at times flag. So it seemed only right and natural that I would sometimes step behind the bar to fill in. One such night, Sunny said, "You look good back here, Timmy. Why don't you stay?"

I knew no more about tending bar than I did about tending sheep, but being asked to bartend at Sunny's was not exactly like asking a season-ticket holder to take the mound for the New York Yankees. Or even for the Toledo Mud Hens. As far as I could tell, I would be opening bottles of beer and occasionally making drinks whose complexity was usually limited to two ingredients. Gin and tonic. Vodka and soda. Scotch and water. So I stayed.

Working at Sunny's did not seem all that different from not working at Sunny's. What Sunny had really meant was, "I'd like you to be with me on this side of the bar but I want you to have the freedom to do as you please." There was no set time that he expected me to arrive or leave, and no such formality as a wage (it was understood that Sunny's was a labor of love, for all involved). The only instruction of substance Sunny gave me was to not drown in the river while the bar was open on a Friday.

In the first months of our friendship I had experienced the contradictory impulses of wanting to bring Sunny a little bit of business by inviting a few friends who I knew shared my ideology when it came to old bars, and wanting to keep

Sunny's to myself—not an uncommon neurosis in New York when one comes upon a place as yet undiscovered by crowds.

Sunny had a self-effacing nature and any sort of promotion of his bar would have been, in his view, a sign of excessive vanity. He would say, "What kind of person would want to blow their own horn?" Now, however, although there were yet moments of great quiet at the bar—one snowy night, the half dozen of us who made it there amused ourselves by revealing each scar we'd earned and telling its backstory—Sunny's was unmistakably becoming busier on its own. Each week it seemed as though there were a couple more customers than the previous Friday.

As we observed this phenomenon, Tone, always commonsensical, raised an issue that Sunny had cheerily ignored. Nothing about Sunny's was lawful. The bar had no liquor license. No business license. No insurance. No certificate of occupancy. No permits at all. They had all been under the name of his uncle and had begun to expire not long after his death. Life had been so sleepy in Red Hook that it did not seem to matter whether these forms were filed. As far as New York City knew, the bar at 253 Conover had ceased to operate with John Balzano's last breath.

It wasn't that Sunny went out of his way to break these regulations—it simply was not in his makeup to investigate them. Except for a brief time during the 1970s after he inherited a small fortune from an heiress and supporter of the arts (she sponsored his creative ambitions while he sated her libido, still active in her ninth decade), he had never possessed a savings account. He had never written a check or charged a credit card. The world of forms and applications and registrations and fees was foreign to him. The bar was an unprosperous affair—it made just enough to sustain itself. The notion that one might want to pay for things like liquor licenses and insurance did not cross his mind. Doing so would have cost more than the bar was taking in. And since we only opened on Fridays, we thought of ourselves more as a social club than a regular business. So Sunny proposed that if we did not charge money for drinks, that is, if we were not engaging in business, the statutes governing bars in the State of New York would not apply to us. It was a logic best not probed too deeply.

The following week Tone hung up a small sign that suggested a three-dollar donation per drink. To further avoid the appearance that we were conducting a business, rather than have customers "donate" their money each time they ordered, with their first drink we would hand them a card on which we had written their name and a tally mark. That card was now their chit and for every drink they ordered the rest of the night, we would add a mark and hope that as they were leaving that night, they would present their card at the bar and we would add up the marks and figure out that evening's donation.

There may have been cleverer ways to circumvent the New York State Liquor Authority, but few that would prove more popular. Customers loved the idea that they were in a legitimate speakeasy (that is, legitimately illegitimate, unlike a few other historic bars in the city that were speakeasies by reputation but not by contemporary practice). They loved the cards, which, on the front sides, were printed with illustrations of nautical terms such as halyards, stern fasts, dolphin strikers, and neap tides.

Above all, they loved the principle behind the cards— trust. Utopian ideals are commonly heard but rarely prac-

ticed in rooms where liquor is consumed, and when coming to Sunny's for the first time, people responded to the honor system in the startled way that city folk respond to the roadside vegetable stand along a rural road where there is no farmer in sight—only a cigar box in which to leave one's payment. In the rare event that a customer left the bar on a Friday night without paying, an envelope containing money and a letter of apology would appear beneath the door during the week.

Being licensed was not the only convention that Sunny did not follow. There was no happy hour. At a bar where drinks were already the same very low price, a happy hour would have been a redundancy. Besides, he considered eight o'clock to be the proper time to open up so as not to disrupt his or anyone else's dinner.

The buyback, the practice of giving a customer a free drink after they have had several rounds, is established practice at all but the most ill-tempered bars, so new customers were often surprised to learn that their fourth drink wasn't on the house. It was not that Sunny was not generous. But to his mind, the act of buying someone a drink should always be a personal gesture—when it became automatic, a policy of reward, it lost its sincerity.

One night I heard him announce that he wanted to buy a man and his son a round and I watched as he set their Budweisers on the bar, came around to their side, took out his wallet and placed a ten-dollar bill on the counter. Later, after they had left and he had returned to our side of the bar, he collected the money and put it in the register.

"Okay, Sunny. I give up. Why? Why are you buying drinks from yourself?"

"Timmy, I do it this way to show that while I may be the owner of the bar, I am paying for this drink out of my pocket," he replied. "I'm not taking it out of the register. It says, 'I want to buy you guys a beer on a personal level. It's not the business buying you a beer—*I'm* buying you a beer.'"

As another customer once observed, Sunny had a thousand ways to make a person feel like a million bucks. This was not a tactic, but a characteristic.

11

That's the Way It Was Around Here

THERE WERE THREE WEAPONS KEPT AT SUNNY'S. TWO nightsticks and a blackjack, all stowed behind the bar. Though serviceable, as their many dents confirmed, they hadn't seen action in recent memory and I thought of them as artifacts from a time when bartenders faced with troublemakers were more inclined to reach down below than for the phone. Over the course of its existence, the bar had been largely spared any real trouble. So far as anyone knew, there had been only one fatal shooting and two holdups in near to eighty years, which has to be some kind of record for a New York City establishment of its type. The shooting had taken place when Sunny was only a boy and if one wanted to be precise, it had been peripheral to the bar—the ice delivery man was ambushed on the front stoop in what turned out to be a vendetta matter. The first robbery, too, had occurred so long ago, there were no living witnesses to give an account.

The more recent one, however, had taken place just a few years before I arrived. Sunny didn't like to talk about it which was, in itself, intriguing, as it was so uncharacteristic of him to hedge on any story in which he played the lead. With some concern for our welfare, mindful that the bar's remoteness would seem to appeal to robbers as much as it did to romantics, I persisted in pressing him for specifics until one night he grudgingly relented.

It had been near closing time. He and the few remaining customers were ordered to the ground by two men with shotguns. They were masked and the only good look Sunny got was from an ankle-high perspective while his face was being pressed against the floor by a gun barrel. He had seen those cuffed Levi's and spotless sneakers before. They belonged to a man whose face he knew from the neighborhood and who had recently been showing up at the bar. Sunny realized he had mistaken casing for run-of-the-mill friendly conversation. The men raged when they looked into the till. "We've been watching this place all night," one of them screamed down at Sunny. "No fucking way you only got seventy-five dollars in the register!" If they had been more observant on their previous visits, they would have made a mental note of the meager crowd and modest liquor selection and come to the sound conclusion that surely there had to be more promising locations for a stickup than Sunny's. The other man issued the standard "Nobody fucking move for ten minutes or they'll get their heads blown off," before backing out the door.

"So, what happened? You told the cops you recognized the pants, the shoes?" I asked. "They went to jail?"

"No, not jail," Sunny replied. "They were . . . how should I put it?" A grin flickered across his face. "Let me just say, they were taken care of, Timmy."

After a pause, his grin widened and an unmistakable, if indecipherable, glint appeared in his eyes. "But I assure you it was done with love."

Love, I was coming to understand, could be a guiding principle even when exacting retribution. And holding up Sunny's could be highly adverse to one's health and, possibly, one's stay on earth.

In my time there would never be cause to grab one of the clubs, and although there were several customers whose appearance gave us a kind of dread, their crimes were usually only against decorum—the overbearing reciters, the notorious swooners, the political orators, the goatish poets, and the occasional senior citizen with a Don Juan delusion. If a person went too far, by, say, inflicting themselves on the entire bar, Sunny would, gently, put the person out by discreetly phoning for a car service and when the cab pulled up out front, tapping the offender on the shoulder and saying, "I'm so sorry to see you're leaving us early tonight but I'm afeared your ride has arrived," and leading the bewildered person out the door. Sunny always observed the principle that if one must ask customers to leave the bar, one should do so in such a way as to leave their dignity intact.

Even when he was confronted with true delinquents, I would never see Sunny unnerved. When someone came to him one night and said, "Sunny—there's a couple guys beating the shit out of somebody on the street," he didn't for a moment consider calling the police but instead walked outside, where two men in the neighboring doorway were taking turns kicking a man lying on his back. Although it was dark, he recognized the men by their size—he guessed the smaller of the two weighed about 250 pounds. They were New Jerseyans and they, too, had only recently begun coming to the bar on a regular basis. They were not subtle about their aspirations in life—once he had seen them open the trunk of their car, revealing a cache of guns inside. Sunny considered them "wannabe wise guys." In his view, a wannabe wise guy was a little more unpredictable, a little more dangerous than an actual wise guy. He also recognized the man being kicked as a neighborhood nuisance, someone asking for trouble wherever he went and who had now found it, perhaps deservedly so. Nevertheless, this beatdown was taking place in what he considered to be his territory, and so he strode over to the New Jerseyan he knew as Spanky.

"You guys want to continue to come here, you got to show respect 'cause this kind of shit don't go," he said. "You do stuff like this here, all you're going to do is give me a reputation so other folks won't want to come. You're going to hurt my business, you're going to hurt my people, you're going to hurt me."

The two men looked uncomfortable. They muttered apologies and promised to stop kicking their victim. They even helped him to his feet.

That was Sunny. He cudgeled villains not with a club but with his words, and did so in a manner they felt compelled to respect.

————

IN ALL THE years I would know him, there would only be two people whose appearance genuinely frightened Sunny; by comparison the wannabe wise guys were innocents abroad. Babes in the wood with Jersey accents. Their names were Jacqueline and Josephine and they were sisters. One walked with a cane, the other with God (when sober), and both filled Sunny with the kind of terror usually reserved for the uncle who shows up uninvited at your wedding with snapshots of his holiday at a swingers' resort in his breast pocket. They were erratic in the way of Joe Pesci's movie characters. They spilled their drinks, their bosoms, and their personalities onto whoever was unlucky enough to be sitting nearby. They considered yelling to be conversation and were as quick to proclaim their amorous intentions for you as they were to denounce your lower anatomy as being inadequate for anything other than emptying your bladder. Naturally they loved Sunny. He never let his true feelings for Jacqueline and Josephine show but instead gave them the kind of attention that they mistook for reciprocation. He could be a very good actor.

Mercifully, Jacqueline and Josephine came to the bar seldom. On one such night, in the small hours when there were only a few people left in the bar, Jacqueline improbably hit it off with a man—he had a rakehell face and was the only customer I knew to wear zoot suits—and she left her sister on a barstool to go sit in a booth with him. Unhappy with the lack of attention or perhaps thinking for a moment she was someplace else entirely, Josephine suddenly pulled her top over her head. She reached back, unclasped her bra, let it slide to the side, and sat on the barstool with her breasts hanging over her stomach like one of Lucian Freud's well-nourished models.

She looked indifferent to the world. I considered the situation: an unpredictable half-nude in the middle of the bar. It was bad, in a way, but I was not then and never would be very good at handling moments like this. I retreated to the farthest corner of the room where the shot glasses are kept, and began re-drying them with a bar towel. I was prepared to let the situation play out.

Suddenly I heard, "Oh, Josephine! Look how beautiful you are! My, my!"

I looked up and saw Sunny standing in the doorway, his hands clasped together as if in appreciation. He had been smoking by himself in the back, where he appeared to have left his senses; beauty was not among the first dozen words that would come to mind for most people to describe Josephine. But Sunny wasn't most people. Josephine, who had been slouching in the way drunkards do, stiffened her back and sat up straight. She lifted her chin. The stool had become her pedestal. She was preening. She was fluttering her eyelashes. She was in a kind of heaven—the heaven that those who are desired feel—and I marveled as I would so many times at Sunny's ability to say the right thing.

"Now, Josephine. I thank you for what you've done, you hear? You've given me this gift of yourself, but I think you should cover yourself up again. Okay?"

Sunny approached her and Josephine swiveled to face him. Her cane, which had been leaning against her barstool, fell to the floor with a crack. Like a guileless doe approaching a mound of corn left by a hunter now perched in a nearby tree, Sunny bent over to pick up Josephine's cane and at that instant Josephine seized him by both ears and yanked his head toward her crotch. "Oh, Sunny!" she shouted. Off bal-

ance, Sunny stumbled forward with a grunt and caught himself on her knees but for an interminable moment, he was
bent at the waist, his head buried in her lap. With a lurch he
righted himself and she let out a triumphant howl. He looked
around unsteadily and said sternly, though not entirely un-
happily, "Josephine! You really have to get dressed now.
Okay? And I'll call you a car. I love you, kid."

"Okay, Sunny," she wailed. "I loooove you, Sunny!"

"That was a close one, Timmy," Sunny said after we had
seen off the two sisters, the man in the zoot suit, and the
other remaining people and locked the door. "I tell you what.
Those are the kind of people, you never know what they're
going to do next. They're cuckoo. The Bimbo Sisters. We
used to have a lot of people like them around here and thank
goodness we don't anymore. That guy sitting in the booth
with Jacqueline—I was going to speak with him, to deter him
from extending himself to her, only because I didn't want to
give them any impetus to come back. But he's the kind of guy
whose head is in his prick. *Pensa col cazzo.* He's not seeing,
he's not thinking, it's just there and he wants it. Reminds me
of myself during various periods in my life, to tell the truth.
When I was young, I spent a considerable amount of time in
the hospital recovering from gangrene and the nurses there
were so beautiful and I was often so horny, I would have to
stick my prick in my belt to keep it locked in. Pour me a
shot."

Sunny sipped his Jameson. I would never develop the
thirst for whiskey that Sunny always seemed to be trying to
slake and I rarely drank late at night. But watching someone
drink alone feels like bad manners and I poured myself just
enough to wet my lips and began sweeping up cigarette butts.

After closing time, the wooden floor would look like a small town ticker-tape parade had passed through earlier.

"Ha! The night of Josephine's tits. Two tits. Have I ever told you about the night of the six tits, Timmy?"

"The night of the six tits? I don't think so, Sunny. It sounds like a creature feature."

"It was, Timmy, only . . . I was the creature!" Sunny exclaimed, his eyes glistening.

"What happened was, this was well before I met Tone and when I was living not next door but in this house over on Dikeman Street when I first moved back to the neighborhood. It was wintertime and I had locked up the store and I was walking toward this club, an unlicensed bar that some friends of mine had opened on the corner of Coffey and Dwight Streets. I think there may be a church there now. Anyways, I get to the other end of that block, the corner of Richards and Coffey, and I'm walking along and I hear *Blam! Blam!* Gunfire coming from the direction of this bar. I look down the street and there are these guys running out of the door and scattering in every direction and some of them are running right toward me. To get away, you see. A lot of guys. And I'm still hearing shots. So this pack of men reaches the spot where I'm standing and they keep running past me and I turn and join them and we're all running together back toward Richards Street! There was snow on the ground and I must have gotten to within about twenty feet of the corner when I hear more shots—*Blam! Blam!*—and I just dove. I dove, Timmy, and I used my body like a fuckin' sled to get to the corner. I lay there for just a moment and then I ducked around a building and when I stood up, wouldn't you know it, these three women are there and they ask me if I'm all right. I say, 'I am' and they ask me where I was going. I say, 'I'm going home now.' And they ask whether they could come with me, have a drink, like that.

"Well, we go to my house and we pour some drinks and it's not too long before they get to talking as to which one was going to have her way with me, aye? Eventually, well, one of them did have her way with me. It was pretty debauched when you consider it. The other two were hooting and slapping me on the ass and when we were done, well, those other two felt left out. They wanted a bit of me, too. I said, 'Thank you, but you see I don't think I'm physically able to do what it is that it is you want me to do.' So one of them had this idea that what I needed was to soak my balls in ice water. This was pre-Viagra, you understand. And that's what we did—she filled a bowl with ice water and she had me squat over this bowl in the kitchen. It didn't work, of course, but I can still hear those ice cubes clinking against the side of the bowl!"

"Thank you for that image," I said.

Sunny giggled until he coughed, and as he regained his composure, I poured him another shot.

"I don't think *The Night of the Six Tits* will be showing at the Saturday matinee anytime soon."

"Timmy, let me tell you—it would be unsuitable for viewers of any age. And I can say that 'cause I was there!"

"Next time someone orders a double highball, I'll let you take care of it."

Sunny smoked in the dark while I took up sweeping again, pondering the night's contradictions. At most other bars, when a customer acted up, they were thrown out. Here, they were paid compliments. The outcome was the same but the distinction being, I decided, that at Sunny's a person wasn't aware that they were being kicked out and they might leave feeling better about themselves than when they first arrived. I had a lot to learn from this man. "Sunny, you're one part psychologist, one part explosives expert," I mused aloud. "Many people wouldn't have the right touch to defuse a time bomb like Josephine."

"Well, certainly, that's my way. Understand, Timmy, it wasn't always like that here at the bar. My family could be tough when it was required. When I was a boy, my father and my uncle used to cash checks for the workers out of the back room, taking a small fee. One night some gangsters, some real heavy hitters from Coney Island, showed up and tried to shake down some of that money from my father. Like they probably did with all the bars down here. Well, just at that moment my father's brother, Uncle Louis, who worked on the harbor patrol, shows up with his partners. We actually called him Gigch. Uncle Gigch, so as to tell him apart from my other uncle Louis, the whistler. They used to tie up at the end of the street and when they'd come in, they'd stash their hats and their guns behind the bar next to the front door. Anyway, my uncle hears what's going on in the back room and he goes back there and says to one of these gangsters, 'You go tell your boss that if we ever see you come into this bar again, trying to strong-arm my family, we're coming down to Coney Island and we're going to wipe out your whole fuckin' family!' He meant it, too. My uncle, what a sweet guy—but he was tough. He worked on the docks for a while and he was one of those men who broke through the Irish hold on the piers down here. And my father . . . fuhgeddaboudit! I remember another time when I was a boy. My father and Uncle John, they would give the guys who worked around here tabs. You know, you don't have any money, you gonna eat, like that. There was one thing they hated most, though, and that was when you didn't have any money and you came to the bar and ate and they put you on a tab and then, when you had money, you ate somewhere else. That was an insult. There was this one guy, a professional fighter. Spanish. It was lunchtime and he came in and he ordered food even though he hadn't paid his bill from the last time. And my father said to him, 'You got some pair of balls. You come here and you want food and you want to put it on the tab. When you got money, you go down the street. I don't mind you going down the street, but you go down the street when you got money and you come here when you got no money?'

"The fighter, he challenged my father. 'Come outside and I'll kick your fuckin' ass!' Something to that degree. Like all of my uncles, my father was small but strong, aye? Nevertheless, I'm watching this take place and I was scared for him. He goes outside and who follows him but my uncle. And they were on that prizefighter like pit bulls. I'm telling you, Timmy, this guy was like a sheep at bay with a couple of pit bulls. My father would give him a shot and he'd turn around and my uncle would give him a shot. I mean, they beat him to the ground. They could have killed him but they taught him a lesson. I was so proud of my father because this guy had always had an attitude and he sort of bragged about it, and the two of them had shown him that no one got away with anything here. And the guy came back later and he paid his bill and nothing was ever said about it again. But people in the neighborhood knew by that, you don't fuck around when you come to this bar. And if you did, well, my father always had the bats. That's the way it was around here."

12

Enrico

I WAS A MAN LIVING TWO LIVES. I HAD TAKEN A JOB AT A magazine on Madison Avenue that was nine miles but many worlds removed from the society of Jacqueline and Josephine, Jersey wannabe wise guys, and the Balzano clan (not to mention nude nighttime swims in the river). At the end of my workweek, when I boarded the subway on Friday evenings, I may as well have been boarding a ship destined for the Ottoman Empire.

Mine was a job that, day to day, resembled many jobs. There were paper jams, ink shortages, frozen screens, and frequent coffee breaks. The work could be engaging, but was often tedious. An eye for detail was required, while a degree of tolerance for manure was helpful. There was a great deal of concern with being ahead of the times. People took pride in knowing the latest. Like all offices, mine had its share of ruthless strivers, shameless self-champions, flagrant narcissists, as well as chronic skirt chasers and serial trouser burglars. Happily, there were also a good many genuine, agreeable, and admirable souls. I divided my days, in roughly equal parts, between the counter of the Grand Central Oyster Bar (for lunch), the pews of St. Patrick's Cathedral (for reading), the aisles of Gotham Book Mart (to pass the time), and my cubicle. I was the obverse of a ruthless striver.

There were several social strata as well as several layers of bosses in this office, and a semi-strict observance of workplace etiquette and hierarchy was expected. At the top, the boss of bosses was a brash, clumsy, and artless man whose principal hobby was collecting skull-and-bone cuff links, which he wore whenever conducting contract negotiations. His locales were Sutton Place, the Royalton Hotel bar, several European capitals where he vacationed every year, and the Four Seasons, where he lunched each afternoon. He was highly set in his ways, and the staff often privately made fun of the narrowness of his habits. He could, after all, afford nearly any whim and yet he returned to the same places—and in the case of the Four Seasons, the same table—day after day. We mocked his lack of imagination to try something new. But in reality, I, too, preferred to go where I was known. I had my own Four Seasons.

Each Friday evening before going to the bar, I unfailingly drove to the opposite end of Red Hook from Sunny's and ate dinner at the same restaurant, Ferdinando's, a Sicilian place a century old. Ferdinando's closed at six o'clock except on Fridays and Saturdays when the owner, Frank Buffa, stayed open till nine. A restaurant that liked to close at six P.M. had a certain kinship to a bar that stayed closed six nights a week. Ferdinando's was the vanishing Brooklyn that is by turns sentimentalized, caricatured, and spoken of in wistful reverie by its émigrés who were now living in the sunshine states. A statue of St. Francis stood high on a shelf, garlands of garlic dangled around a cast-iron stove, and the walls were hung with yellowed Palermo newspapers, a map of Sicily, daguerreotypes of Italian cities, as well as snapshots of a younger Mr. Buffa diving to block a soccer ball and posing with bombshell Maria Grazia Cucinotta.

Although there were many other restaurants between my house and Sunny's, I had always been a person of loyalty and custom once I found a place I liked. So each Friday I would meet with the same several friends at Ferdinando's. Mr. Buffa soon asked us to call him Frank. We were so dependable that he would hold the center table for us.

Frank was a slightly melancholy, if restless-looking, man with an unfeigned sense of hospitality. He spoke heavily accented English although he had been in America since 1971. One evening while I was waiting for my friends to arrive, he settled into the chair across from me and casually mentioned that earlier that day Luciano Pavarotti had had two servings of his tripe.

"Pavarotti was here? At Ferdinando's?" I asked, incredulous.

"No, no, Teem. He send his driver. His driver, he pick up the tripe," Frank replied.

This interested me very much and Frank very little. Although his restaurant looked like the kind of place one might expect to hear the death scene aria from *La Traviata* upon entering, the last time Frank had voluntarily listened to opera was the year before he left Italy, when a beautiful American took him to see *The Flying Dutchman* in Rome. After ten minutes he decided that Wagner was more unbearable than any woman was desirable, and he stood up and left her forever. He had only mentioned the Pavarotti incident to me because it made him proud that a famous person had eaten his tripe that day. A famous Italian, no less.

By this point, I was a lay historian in all matters Red Hook and I told Frank that Luciano Pavarotti was not the first tenor of the Metropolitan Opera to send an emissary rather than come to Red Hook himself. He shrugged as if to say, "So? What's the big deal?" but I ignored his indifference—being his most regular customer has some privileges.

The Black Hand first appeared in America in 1903 when a wealthy Red Hook dock builder named Nicolo Cappiello received a series of extortion letters. Such letters were not especially unusual, as blackmail was widely practiced in Italian districts. What made these particular letters notable were their signatures: "La Mano Nera." The Black Hand. In Italy, there had been rumors of a criminal society with that name for years but this was the first instance of it appearing in connection with a crime in America.

When Cappiello didn't comply with the letters' demands, he was visited by several men who introduced themselves as representatives of the Order of the Black Hand. Cappiello didn't yield to this more ominous, face-to-face approach either, and instead went to the police, who would eventually succeed in entrapping the blackmailers.

The newspaper accounts of the trial were sensationalistic and made other would-be blackmailers realize how effective the idea of a secret criminal society could be in evoking menace. Soon immigrants in other Italian quarters such as East Harlem, Williamsburg, and the Lower East Side were receiving letters from the Black Hand.

Often written in a florid style, the letters would begin politely enough, with, say, "Honorable Sir," but end with threats such as, "Pay up or we will blow you to atoms." They were signed variously by the Society, the Order, or the Company of the Black Hand and they were typically illustrated

Alfred J. Young Collection, N.Y.C.

with skulls, daggers, crosses, and . . . black hands. But unlike those in the Cappiello case, many of these letters were not empty threats. Dynamite was easily stolen from construction sites, and bombings became the preferred method of coercion of the early Black Handers. Newspapers regularly and alarmingly reported on storefronts and homes and occasionally their inhabitants being blown up.

Soon the press began to credit all violent crimes committed by Italians to the Black Hand and imply that Southern Italians, who comprised nearly all Italian immigration to America, were a criminal race of people. The extortion letters and the uncertainty of whether the Black Hand really existed inspired a degree of hysteria that is hard to fathom today. While some investigators concluded that all one needed to be a Black Hand conspirator was a fountain pen and paper, others believed in a vast fraternity of criminals whose tentacles stretched from Calabria to Chicago.

It would be a dozen years before it became clear that the Black Hand had never been a codified and hierarchical organization such as the Mafia in Sicily, that it had not even been an alliance of criminals but instead simply a criminal technique, and the use of the name and symbol faded by the time the First World War began and disappeared almost entirely by 1920.

Red Hook would only have been a footnote in the history of the Black Hand, as the place where the phenomenon first appeared in America, in the way the Ed Sullivan Theater is a footnote in the story of the Beatles, were it not for the fact that it was also in Red Hook that the most notorious, and entertaining, Black Hand extortion attempt was made.

In 1910, several days before Metropolitan Opera tenor

Enrico Caruso, then the preeminent Italian in America, was to appear at the Brooklyn Academy of Music to sing in *La Gioconda,* he received a letter that read, "Senor Caruso. You tomorrow at the hour of two will be stopped by a boy and you must deliver $15,000. You think right to not say anything to nobody. C.D.M. †" The initials stood for Compagnia della Morte, the Company of Death, and the black cross was a known symbol of the Black Hand.

The next day Caruso took his customary afternoon walk outside his home in the Knickerbocker Hotel on 42nd Street, shadowed by detectives. Soon, the tenor received a second letter that read, "Senor Caruso: You yesterday went in the company of two policemen. The boy could not make salute. Tonight, just at the hour of six, you must leave in one bag the sum of $15,000 under the stairs where the factory is on the corner of Sackett and Van Brunt Street, Brooklyn. You think good and don't fail. If you fail, Saturday night will not pass that you will pay." Leaving no doubt to their identity, the blackmailers signed this letter with the more formal La Mano Nera Compagnia della Morte—the Black Hand Company of Death.

Caruso decided that Red Hook was no place for a grand opera tenor to be in the middle of the night and instead sent a double, along with several undercover police officers, to deliver a decoy packet of money. When two men were seen arriving at the designated corner, glancing around suspiciously before fleeing, they were tackled by the detectives who had been hiding nearby. The Black Handers were revealed to be two Red Hookers named Antonio Cincotti and Antonio Misiani.

The following day, upon hearing of the arrest of the two

Antonios, Caruso smote his chest and blew kisses at the pink lilies that decorated his hotel suite and declared, "The Black Hand scares me not. Caruso says 'Ha-ha!' to the Black Hand. Should they open fire on me in the theater, I will shoot them down like flies. Caruso, he is always armed. Never is he without his revolver and his sword cane!"

The great illeist sang for another ten years while Cincotti, the leader of the plot, served a short prison sentence at Sing Sing and soon after his release was shot dead, a few doors down from Ferdinando's, upon leaving a nearby movie house.

When I finished my story and began gathering my jacket and cap to go open up the bar, Frank shrugged and said only, "You know who else like-a my food? Frank Sinatra. He once order an entire platter of arancini."

"Sinatra, Frank?" Now I was impressed. I had been listening to *In the Wee Small Hours* since my third or fourth broken romance. "Sinatra ate here?"

"No, he send his driver, too. He send his driver from Long Island, I think. I don't-a know what he was doin' in Long Island but I know he want my rice balls."

It seemed not even Sinatra would come to Red Hook.

13

Radio Days

WHEN SUNNY WAS A BOY, THERE WERE TWO MEN IN Brooklyn named Leo who also had the moniker "Lip." One was Leo the Lip, the bellicose player-manager of the pennant-winning Dodgers, and the other was a luckless soul who lived in the Point and who was known throughout the neighborhood as Lip-Lip Leo. Though he was a grown man, Lip-Lip Leo was tiny and he had dwarf-like features. Stubs for fingers. Something was broken in his mind and when a fire engine or an ambulance or a garbage truck drove by, Lip-Lip Leo would run after it like a territorial dog. No one knew why he did this. And when he saw the boys in the neighborhood start to pick up stones, he would run, too, because he knew they were getting ready to chase him, chanting, "Lip-Lip Leo! Lip-Lip Leo! There goes Lip-Lip Leo!" To be Leo the Lip—Leo Durocher, the Dodgers' manager— was to live a charmed existence in wartime Brooklyn; to be Lip-Lip Leo was to curse existence every morning.

Red Hook was filled with wretches and outcasts like Lip-Lip Leo. Some were shunned for their bizarre if harmless behavior or for misshapen bodies. Others had allowed whatever light they had been born with to be extinguished by heavy drinking. Their homes smelled like boiled socks and week-old hot dogs. They argued and cursed and drank in front of their kids, who came to the Balzanos' house for a few hours of normalcy.

Sunny's parents had a stable marriage and they were loving to their children. Theirs was the kind of home where the smell of food cooking was appetizing. It wasn't a well-to-do home. There were few of those in Red Hook. After the largest public housing project in Brooklyn, the Red Hook Houses, was completed in the late 1930s for the families of dockworkers, Sunny looked at the amenities—hot water and elevators and courtyards that included playgrounds and lawns—with wonder. His home had no running hot water and in the summertime, showering to Sunny meant going up to the roof with a bar of soap when it rained. In the winter, his shins were perpetually bruised from having to carry the sloshing bucket of heating kerosene up from the basement. He rarely owned more than one pair of shoes at a time and when the leather wore clean through on the bottom, he stuffed them with newspapers to keep his feet dry. One of those shoes with a hole in the sole is sitting on a shelf in the bar today like a hallowed relic. Every year, the week before Easter, his mother would take him to Fulton Street in downtown Brooklyn to buy one suit, two pairs of pants, and a fedora, which had to last him until the following Easter. Every Saturday she gave him one new pair of thin socks, which he was to wear for one week before throwing them away.

What he lacked in possessions was compensated by a sense of family and a warmth to his home life. There were five apartments in the two buildings that his grandfather Antonio had bought, and in each lived a grandparent or an aunt or uncle with a spouse and family. On holidays it felt as though there were five homes to visit. There would be five Christmas trees to admire, five kitchen tables to sit at, five radios turned to *Gang Busters* or *The Shadow* or *Jack Armstrong* or *The Battle of the Baritones*. When the extended family came together for holidays, they played cards, did impersonations, and put on short comedy sketches. The house was full of music. Ralph, Sunny's father, would play the guitar and his mother would ask him to sing "A Little on the Lonely Side." Ralph would also sing "Just a Gigolo"—because that's how he liked to think of himself. Sunny's uncle Louis, the one who had gone to whistling school in Italy, would play the mandolin and twitter and tweet like a sparrow and sing Italian popular songs such as "Funiculi Funicula" and "Marechiare."

The world beyond the doorstep was at once perilous and thrilling. There were no playgrounds at this end of Red Hook; there was no grass at all. The ball fields were the flat roofs of the warehouses on the neighboring street—low dividing walls served as outfielders, and singles, doubles, and triples were measured by which successive wall one could hit the ball over. A home run had to reach the street. The local swimming pool was the gut of a partly sunken wooden ship across the street where a shipyard had once been. The fishing hole was the harbor. In the summer Sunny and some of his brothers and cousins would launch a plywood skiff with a five-horsepower motor from the end of Conover Street and cross the shipping lanes to the backside of the Statue of Liberty, where there was a graveyard for old ferryboats. The ferries were entirely submerged but at low tide one could walk on the highest parts, then only ankle-deep under water. The wrecks had become spawning grounds for crabs that lived there in great numbers, and the boys threw nets and scalloped the crabs from along nearby pilings and filled up V-shaped bushel baskets. Recrossing the bay to Red Hook, they kept lookout for the dangerous wakes, known as willies, created by passing tugs and ships. "Here come the willies!" they would yell and shift their weight around the boat. They hauled the crabs back to Red Hook and Sunny's father boiled them up in the bar, laid newspapers on the sidewalk, and handed out hammers and pliers, and they would eat crabs till they were tired of picking them. What remained was served up in soup at the bar.

It was on the piers that Sunny had his earliest encounters with death. His father's brother, Uncle Gigch, the harbor patrolman, periodically came to shore with bodies he had found in the water tied onto the back of his patrol boat. The first corpse that Sunny saw up close was one of these bodies, gorged eels emerging from its hollows. Sex, too, was on view at the piers as older boys took part in group masturbation circles—the brazenness of their public act transfixing and repelling him.

AFTER A YEAR in public school, Sunny was sent to the School of the Visitation, Red Hook's Catholic school. He was a poor student and his knuckles were always raw. To the Irish nuns he was a guinea who stubbornly refused to learn how to read and write out of sheer guineaness. Dyslexia wasn't a recognized condition and he was made to feel stupid for his illiteracy and ashamed to be Italian. Even when he excelled in a subject, such as art, he was made to feel inferior. The teacher would assign perspective drawings, simplistic exercises such as rendering train tracks disappearing in the distance, and Sunny would draw those tracks from multiple perspectives at once. The teacher would take the artwork from the hands of the Irish kids, the German kids, but when Sunny would approach to turn in his work, she would have him leave it on her desk to avoid making contact with him.

When he failed to learn the catechism in order to make First Holy Communion, Sunny's mother went to see the parish priest, Father Casey, to ask whether he could be allowed to take the test again. Father Casey was an intimidating man, feared by the students and nuns alike. Before Sunny's mother had finished her entreaty, Father Casey held his palm up in her face and shouted in his Irish brogue, "He took the test once and he failed it! He should have studied harder and you should have taken the responsibility!"

Sunny's mother started pleading with him. "Please, Father Casey," she began.

"I am not going to give in," he yelled. "He took the test and he failed it and that's it!"

Sunny grabbed his mother by her skirt.

"Come on, Mom," he said. "Come on. Let's just go." But she kept on imploring the priest, who looked down at her icily.

"Fuck him, Mom!" Sunny finally cried. "Fuck him!"

She turned to him with a horrified look on her face and whispered, "But, Sunny, he's a priest. . . ."

Sunny's voice was pitching higher with every word. "Fuck him! He can't talk to my mother like that! Fuck him!"

Sunny was not supposed to say "fuck," not to a priest, not to any adult. Cussing in front of one's family, let alone a priest, was something one simply did not do. It was like opening the door to the toilet while someone was in there. His mother said "shit" once and she apologized for a day. Only one person in his family was allowed to say "fuck," and then only on special occasions such as Christmas or Easter. During family gatherings for such holidays, Uncle Gigch would take out a comb and sweep Sunny's younger brother Frank's hair across his forehead, then hand him the comb to hold over his upper lip, and then Uncle Gigch would announce the arrival of Il Duce and Der Führer and he would puff his chest and lower lip out and begin a demagogic oratory in Italian while Frank goose-stepped in circles around him, bellowing in a mock German accent, "YOUFUCKING-SCHWEINEHUNDFUCKINGDRECKSKERLYOUFUCKINGFUCKER!"

Sunny never traveled to Manhattan and the only other neighborhood he knew outside of Red Hook was Coney Island, where he would visit his grandfather at the Steeplechase circus. What little he knew of the world beyond his vision he learned from the radio and from the newsreels at the Pioneer Theater, which were dominated by battlefield reports from various fronts. When the war had first begun, Sunny mistook the lights of Staten Island for those of Europe and when he heard about the destruction that was taking place there, he gazed across the water many hours wondering how it was that the people there could not flee across that short span of water to the safety of Red Hook?

Soon blue and eventually gold stars began appearing in

the windows of families with husbands or sons in the service
and his mother hung blackout curtains in their apartment and
his father hung them over the two windows of the bar and
headlight hoods were welded onto cars and collection piles
for tin cans appeared on the street corners. Sunny knew the
names of all the great generals—Bradley, MacArthur, LeMay.
The mailman brought prized letters from his uncle John, who
was fighting in France, and from his uncle Tony, who had
been sent to the South Pacific. When bombers like the B-25
flew overhead, the houses would shake from the noise of their
piston engines. Vigilant grandmothers scanned the harbor
with binoculars for U-boats at first light and searchlights
swept the sky after nightfall. Each time air-raid warnings
sounded every other week, Sunny imagined the Eastern
Seaboard—and Red Hook—had finally come in range of the
Luftwaffe's Junkers.

The war preoccupied his imagination. He had his own air
force, a flock of pigeons that he kept on the roof, and dogfights over Germany were reenacted in the skies over Red
Hook by warring neighborhood coops. Various breeds—
homers, tumblers, fantails—stood in for Mustangs and Spit-
fires and Messerschmitts. The outcome of the skirmishes was
more benign than those taking place in European skies, re-
sulting only in the capture of enemy birds. When a pigeon
strayed from a passing flock, Sunny would throw his own
flock up in an attempt to dupe the bird into changing alle-
giances. And when an intact flock flew by overhead, he would
first throw a tumbler pigeon, hoping that it would fly directly
into the invading band and, true to its name, tumble backward, dividing the flock in two. He would then release the
rest of his flock with the hope that in the confusion some of

the separated birds would merge and return to roost with his pigeons.

The U.S. Navy berthed ships directly down the street from the bar and when the war ended, some of the ships were decommissioned and sent to scrap yards, leaving behind scores of lifeboats stacked into pillars on shore. Sunny and his brothers soon discovered that the boats still contained ration boxes and flare guns and for months after V-J Day one would periodically hear a whoosh in the evening and look up to see a glowing red fireball suspended from a tiny parachute drifting over the rooftops, not a declaration of distress but just of life itself.

14

Cézanne's Fruit

"**H**OW CAN WE CALL OURSELVES A SAILOR BAR IF WE don't even have a boat?"

This was one of Sunny's standard laments and though my standard reply was to point out that there were very few actual sailors or ship workers of any kind among the current clientele and that we were less a sailor bar than a retired sailor bar, he brought it up time and again. He could be stubborn with his fixations, and in his view, as long as we were boatless, we were cowboys without horses, firemen without a truck.

I already knew Sunny to make quite a few pronouncements that, while uttered in sincerity, were unlikely to ever come to anything. For instance, occasionally visitors from abroad found their way to the bar and befriended Sunny. By the excitement with which foreigners sometimes greeted Sunny upon meeting him, I concluded that in international circles, Sunny's was already as famous a bar as Harry's New

York Bar in Paris or Havana's Floridita. When it came time for them to say goodbye, Sunny would say, "Do me a kindness and write down your address." And with unfeigned conviction, he promised that he was going to reciprocate the favor they had done to him in visiting the bar by paying them a visit in return. There was no doubt in either the visitors' minds or in Sunny's mind that he would be booking an airline ticket in short order to do so. There is a painter in Copenhagen, a short-order cook in Luxor, a tailoress in Rome, each waiting to this day for Sunny's imminent arrival. Although Sunny never made a promise without fully believing in it himself, on his bedside dresser was an ever-growing pile of notes on which were written the names and addresses of people he no longer could put a face to.

So I didn't take this latest notion of his procuring a boat any more seriously than his emphatic declaration that he would be spending New Year's in Osaka.

One day late in the summer, I came home to a message on my answering machine: "Timmy, it's Sunny. It pleases me to let you know that the bar now has its boat! And might I say that it is a vessel of the grandest kind. I think you are going to be quite impressed. Okay, bye for now."

I went to visit Sunny that week to see his new acquisition. He had often talked about the assortment of boats that had been in his family when he was younger—saltwater cruisers, rum boats, simple skiffs for fishing Jamaica Bay—and knowing of his love for all things historical, I imagined I might be greeted by a vintage wooden Lyman hardtop, a prewar Gar Wood runabout. But instead of directing me to the small mooring around the corner from the bar, he led me into the backyard and with a flourish, presented the new bar boat—a yellow, sit-on-top two-seater kayak that had more than a passing resemblance to a banana lying on its back. I was amused rather than disappointed. I praised this latest whimsy of his and said we had to get it out on the water as soon as possible. Yet fall arrived and the kayak languished unused in the yard where Sunny would, on occasion, and with great pride, take indulgent customers to show off the "bar's boat" sitting in dry dock. Sunny had never been one for needless physical exertion.

Finally, during the second week of November, I called Sunny and suggested we make an excursion before winter set in. The following day was Veterans Day, I had the day off from work, and it was supposed to be bright and mild for the time of year. Knowing the forecast was as far as my planning would go. I didn't look up the tide table or inquire whether Sunny owned a flare gun, a whistle, or any sort of foul-weather gear. I didn't prepare for any eventuality other than us paddling around in the harbor, having a good time of it, and returning when we had had enough. Weeks earlier I had taken a walk up the suspension cables to the top of the Brooklyn Bridge in the dead of night. It was a rite of passage for certain kinds of fools in those days. I had brought along a friend, a climber tutored on Mounts Denali and Rainier—and perhaps I had come to think of Sunny not as a man who had just begun drawing Social Security but as another peer ready to go on an escapade impetuously. Even poor judgment seemed to be a quality we admired in each other.

When I arrived, Sunny was still getting dressed. He and Tone lived in the apartment that had belonged to Uncle John. Sunny had inherited all of his late uncle's mid-century furnishings, and their dining room and kitchen resembled a very cluttered version of the set of *I Love Lucy*. It was plain that this was their most private space, as it lacked any pretense. Art supplies and sketchbooks were heaped layers deep on seemingly every surface, and clothing hung from all available handles and knobs. While Tone brewed me coffee and herself tea, we watched as Sunny pulled on two pairs of pants over his long johns, a pullover, a sweater, a down jacket, a pair of wool socks that he "waterproofed" with two plastic bags, and his boots. As a finishing touch, he placed a fur-lined leather flyer's cap on his head.

"Sunny, do you expect us to be crossing the Bering Strait today?"

"Actually, Timmy, unless you had another destination in mind, I thought we might head to Jurassic Park. You know where that is, right?"

"On the big screen?"

"Nye. It's down in the direction of Bay Ridge, though not anywhere that far. There used to be a pier there that since burnt down. It had been so hot in that fire, that all the bones, all the steel frame, bent and twisted. It looks like the skeleton of a dinosaur so I call it Jurassic Park. In some ways, the bones of that pier are more exciting to me as an artist than any sculpture you might find in a museum."

In the mid-nineties, there was a small contingent of canoeists in Red Hook who called themselves the Red Hook Navy. One would occasionally see them late in the day, pushing off the pier and disappearing into the shimmer as they paddled toward the Statue of Liberty. Some Fridays they would come in the bar and boast a little about where they had been. The far side of Governors Island. Up Buttermilk Channel to the Brooklyn Bridge. A neighborhood carpenter took a date to Battery Park at the southern tip of Manhattan, where they rented a space in a parking lot for their canoe while they went to dinner. I had had a vague idea about re-tracing their expedition, but Sunny made a collapsing pier sound more exciting than anything found in Manhattan. "Sure, Sunny. Let's make a journey to Jurassic Park."

We slipped into a pair of life jackets I had brought along as an afterthought and carried the boat from the backyard through the bar, pausing by the front door underneath the photograph of Sunny's uncle, beaming from the deck of the *Lieutenant Ronaghan*. "If Uncle Gigch was here for this, Timmy . . . I can see him right now shaking his head at me. He was always warning us about the river."

The trouble with offhand foreshadowing remarks is that we don't understand their significance at the time.

Outside, the sky was cloudless and the air crisp, the kind of fall morning that is usually the province of New England but finds its way down to the city on occasion. We raised the kayak above our heads and walked down the middle of the street toward the harbor. In those days, one was about as likely to encounter a car on Conover Street as to collide with another twosome portaging a boat.

We dropped the kayak into the water and climbed aboard; I took the bow, Sunny the rear. The tip of Conover was quickly behind us and the water widened and our moods matched the expansiveness of the bay that opened up ahead.

"Timmy! It's amazing to see the harbor like this. To see Red Hook from the water. I haven't done anything like this since I was, oh, maybe fifteen years old. In fact, I feel like I'm fifteen years old. You wouldn't believe how this place has changed. We got the harbor to ourselves now but back then the river was so busy, ten minutes didn't go by without ships warning other ships where they were. You had barges, ferries, navy ships. Nowadays they could be unloading ten ships with cargo twenty times as great as they were unloading in those days and you'd never even know it was happening. You don't see it anymore. There's no activity, there's no music, there's no sound, there's no smell. You used to smell the coffee beans in the burlap sacks. You used to smell the produce. It seemed like ships from every nation in the world used to come through here."

"Why do I get the feeling you must have gotten into some shit back then?" I yelled over my shoulder.

"Oh, fuhgeddaboudit! Literally, we did! The docks are where we learned to swim and all the sewage from their terlets came out of the hulls of the ships tied up down here. We would draw straws for who'd break the ice. What that meant was that those who lost the draw would jump in and push the shit out of the way and we would swim in that circle. We developed an immunity to disease that way, I suppose. Kids in other neighborhoods got vaccinations. We just swam in sailor shit."

I smelled tobacco and I knew without turning around that Sunny had stopped paddling to light a cigarette. He considered every moment an opportune time to smoke, even when his hands weren't free. It was pleasant to talk like this over the splashing of the water, unhurried and with no real itinerary. We were on a holiday.

"Did you climb up on the ships?"

"I'd like to say yes, but no—I was afraid. You couldn't actually climb up the ropes because they used to have rat protection. Line guards. But we would dare each other to run up the gangplanks. Not on the banana ships, though. They were taboo because we were told they were full of tarantulas. A kid's imagination is such that you believed it. One bite, you're dead! But one Thanksgiving, my brother Frank and his friend Bobby Peterson, they snuck up on a ship and they went to the galley and they grabbed the turkey and they came running out the back of the ship with the chef and sailors chasing them and us watching from the dock. And they threw the turkey overboard and just dove in after it, like that! Sad if you think about it, it being Thanksgiving, but to us it was just antics. And I know you know about antics, Timmy. You don't climb the fuckin' Brooklyn Bridge if you don't know antics."

"I never stole a turkey from hungry sailors."

We had left Red Hook's shorefront of warehouses and a police impound lot behind and were passing the mouth of the Gowanus Bay, an inlet at the easterly end of Red Hook. The swells were several feet deep, nothing like the minor chop close to shore. The wind had gotten sharper and we were undeniably working a little harder to make headway. Our progress told me that Sunny was reacquainting himself with his paddle after his smoke. We wigwagged onward, vacillating between a southeasterly and northeasterly course when, suddenly, Sunny let out a cry. I turned and saw his flyer's hat in the water drifting fifteen, and quickly twenty, feet behind us.

"Let it go, Timmy," Sunny said.

"We can get it, Sunny."

I began pulling hard on one side and Sunny followed my lead, reverse-paddling on the opposite side, and in the course of a couple minutes, we had turned the boat rather deftly, paddled back to his cap, snatched it out of the water, and resumed our original approximate bearing.

"My mother, who don't even drive, couldn't have parked a car any better than the job we just did."

This statement made no sense on a number of levels but I didn't disagree with him. Sunny was beaming and we were both feeling highly pleased with ourselves, brimming with overconfidence at our seafaring abilities. Jurassic Park, ferryboat graveyards, the Balzano ancestral home of Calabria. Anything seemed within reach that day. It's at moments like these, the self-satisfied ones, that we are most prone to forgetting that Vanna White is always waiting in the wings.

When we rolled, we rolled as smoothly as a bottle rolling off a tabletop. There was no struggle, no desperate attempt to throw our weight to one side, no yelp. We had been upturned as if by a great hand and unexpectedly dumped into the late-autumn water, and the boat, our splendid bar boat, was drifting upside down several feet away. I looked for Sunny at once and saw him floating a couple arm-lengths away, just out of reach of the hull.

I yelled for him to hold on and, gripping the overturned boat to keep it from being borne away, pulled my way hand over hand until I was treading water in front of him and drew him toward me. His gray mane of hair drifted on the surface around him and he had a wild-eyed look on his face, like a water god who had grown old overnight and lost his powers. His head was tilted back as he struggled to keep his face above the waves. His woolen socks, his long underwear, his two pairs of pants, his pullover, his sweater, and his down jacket absorbed water better than a roll of Bounty.

I said, "Sunny, we've got to try and flip this back. Now. We're both going to push up at the same time, okay?"

He nodded and we shoved at the boat futilely for a few seconds. We had no leverage and the waves slapped the up-turned hull as if to counterpunch our efforts. Sunny let his head hang back again and a resigned look came over his face. I slipped one hand under his armpit.

"Sunny! Sunny! Listen to me. We're going to be all right."

"Timmy, I don't think I'm going to make it. There were so many more paintings I wanted to paint."

Sunny would be an artist to the end.

I looked around. Though it was hard to judge from the waterline, we seemed to be about a quarter mile from shore, a distance I was sure I could cross if I were alone and slipped off my life jacket. I had returned alive from enough nighttime swims to know my abilities. But with Sunny, that short stretch of water seemed an impossible distance to cross. There were no ships in sight and even if there had been, our voices wouldn't have carried far. We were on our own.

I treaded water and looked up at the hull again. A notch ran along the keel.

"Sunny, see that groove? I'm going to push you up and you're going to get your fingers in there and you're going to hold on while I get around to the other side."

I shoved Sunny upward and he clawed at the hard plastic until he managed to wedge his fingers into the notch. Letting go, I made my way around to the other side until I came back alongside him. Lunging out of the water, I grabbed his wrists before falling back, catapulting him up and onto the boat. I quickly hauled myself up and sat next to Sunny, who lay face-down and entirely still, his legs still partially submersed. He had become very quiet, as though he had fallen into a trance. I patted his back and said someone would see us. "We'll be all right, Sunny. We're okay. We're okay."

The minutes passed and we drifted in silence. Boethius would have had something to say about this. He knew about dire straits, writing his most famous work, *The Consolation of Philosophy*, while in a cell awaiting his execution. Up to that point, things had been good for him. Born into a high family in the final days of the Roman Empire, he'd spent his career interpreting philosophy, translating scholarly texts from the Greek, involving himself in ecclesiastic debates— having the time of his life—until some envious bureaucrats defamed him to the monarch whom he served. Facing a grisly death, Boethius imagines himself visited by a woman personifying philosophy, and the two have a late-night bull session. They hit all the big topics that might preoccupy a sixth-century philosopher—predestination, free will, the nature of virtue, the meaning of justice. Weighty and abstruse matters, but what the Everyman in the Middle Ages took away from *Consolation* is the idea that we are always subject to fortune's wheel. One moment you're on top of the world, giving your acceptance speech, and by the afternoon, the wheel has turned a quarter notch. Perhaps only an eighth. If you're lucky, it's only inched ahead and prosperity will stick around for a while, but don't be fooled. Earthly life is instability and the only recourse is to have a balanced view of things. Never get too high or too low on yourself.

I looked at the distant Verrazano Bridge and imagined the cars, invisible to us, crossing the span, their drivers listening to Steve Somers or books on tape or searching their wallets for their toll money or looking at the horizon of the open ocean and wishing they were on their way to some place different entirely. All those people crossing that span of sky were oblivious to the struggle of the two tiny specks far below. That *all* of New York was unaware of us, that the great engine of the city kept humming without pause, seemed incredible.

I scanned the shoreline again, this time spotting a police cruiser where earlier there had only been an empty pier. I began waving, at first to no apparent effect, until the driver's side window rolled down and an arm emerged and briefly acknowledged us. I gave Sunny an excited squeeze and he briefly lifted his head like a turtle roused from sleep. "It'll only be a little while now," I told him. But we continued our slow drift, the current sloshing us and taking us moment by moment just a little farther from the pier, with no sign from the patrol car that a rescue operation was under way or that its occupants were in any way interested in our little caper. I began waving again. Once more, the arm came out of the car window, returned my wave, and withdrew.

What the fuck, I thought.

If we made it out of this, I vowed that I was going to track down the officers in the cruiser and present them with an anthology of modern British poetry, dog-eared to Stevie Smith's "Not Waving but Drowning."

EVENTUALLY, FROM A distance, the thump of a helicopter arose, and not long after it made a single low pass over, we saw a boat make a beeline toward us. An NYPD harbor unit pulled up alongside and first the two of us, and then the kayak, looking humiliatingly toy-like, were pulled aboard by the crew. The senior officer asked, "What did you think you were doing out there?" Shaking his head in disgust, another asked, "What kind of fools are you?" A third exclaimed, "Sunny! Is that you, Sunny?"

Standing sheepishly in the stern, we were brought to the pier, where the patrol car had meanwhile been joined by a fire truck, an ambulance, and, inexplicably, a group of prisoners who had been ushered out of their school bus and who, like manacled sightseers, were now peering at us no less intently than if we had been recaptured Alcatraz escapees. On shore, the motley group of jailers, prisoners, land and water officers, firemen, and paramedics huddled around us while we stripped to our underwear and pulled blankets around our shoulders.

Embarrassed by all the attention, Sunny asked whether a cab couldn't be called to take us home. He fished a soggy hundred-dollar bill from a pocket and held it up as proof we weren't entirely down and out. A murmur of appreciation passed through the prisoners. But the medics dutifully talked us into the ambulance and once we were there they talked us into being hooked up to heart monitors. Soon, Sunny and I were left alone again and sat facing each other, EKG cables hanging from our bare chests. He had bummed a cigarette from the ambulance crew, which he smoked with a slightly enraptured expression. Not so long ago in New York you could smoke both in bars and ambulances.

"When I heard that helicopter, I thought to myself, 'They sent the Italians to come get us.'"

"What?"

"The Italians, Timmy. Wop-wop-wop."

A siren's wail broadcast our trip to a hospital in Brooklyn Heights, cars, we imagined from the back, scattering in our path. To our bewilderment, our arrival was treated as an actual emergency and we were placed on gurneys and wheeled into the ER. The orderlies left us side by side in a curtained corner, unsure of what would be done to us next. "I wish they weren't making such a fuss about us, Timmy."

A nurse soon came over and announced that she needed to take Sunny's core temperature. He opened his mouth but she shook her head slowly with a slight smile. "Other end," she said in a cheery Caribbean accent. Sunny began shaking his head, insisting that he had caught such a fright when the boat tipped over that he shat in his pants. The ruse did not work and with a woebegone expression, Sunny rolled onto his side and I looked away. It would be my turn soon enough.

As we waited for our temperatures to rise over the next several hours, doctors came into the emergency room and asked to see the rescued sailors. We had our pictures taken with Wanda, our nurse. We played along with their amusement at our misadventure, but Sunny was restless. He repeatedly asked Wanda whether "the PMS truck" would be taking us home any time soon and she rolled her eyes and tsk-tsked as she went about her duties. The PMS truck was the kind of truck only Sunny could see, in the same way that only Sunny had a prescription to the *New York Post* and only Sunny was put under by an amnesiologist when going into surgery.

I wanted to sleep but Sunny was talking quietly from his bed next to mine, half to me, half to himself, and I listened with my eyes closed. I always tried to listen when Sunny talked.

"Those officers on the harbor patrol, they reminded me of these three guys on the harbor unit that used to come whenever they had a chance to tie up down by the bar. This was a few years before I met you, Timmy. I suppose they'd seen that photograph of my uncle Gigch in his uniform on his boat through the window. They loved to come in there because it gave them a sense of what it was like in the old days. A lot of verbiage was exchanged. One of them was a young guy, strong. Close-cropped hair, kind of muscular. Kenny was his name. Ken Hansen. Really, what a sweet nature he had. A lot of the guys on the water patrol have a certain friendliness that earth police don't have. If you notice on the water, people on boats, they wave. 'How are you? Did you catch anything today?' If you're marooned, they're the first ones to help you. They tend to do more. If they're not as tough as can be, they're as gentle as can be.

"Anyway, one day the crew came in without Kenny and I asked about him. They were like in a state of mourning and they told me that he had drowned in the harbor. The story I got was that he'd volunteered for mock rescue for a television crew. He volunteered to be the victim. And from what I understand, they asked him if he would mind very much taking off his life vest to make it look real and so he did. And he dove in and treaded water and then disappeared. Imagine, a grown man, strong swimmer. But it's so easy to get caught in those undercurrents and they're running every which way. That's how unpredictable water is. You swim off the piers, Timmy, the way we used to when I was a boy. That isn't like swimming in the ship lane, but I do worry about you every time you disappear from the bar at night.

"I tell you, I was ready to go today. I was sure I was a goner and I wanted to make it quick. I was ready to slip out of that vest and take a big gulp of water. But then I thought of how Tone and my mother would have to identify my body after we'd been found, perhaps weeks from now. All black and blue. And I realized, I couldn't do it. In fact, I thought of how we'd be discolored in the way Cézanne's fruit was discolored in his still lifes. His paintings, they incorporated the changing color, the bruising of the fruit as it rotted. Strange, in that moment, I thought of my lover, my mother, and Cézanne."

With that he, or I, or both of us, fell asleep.

LATE IN THE day we were handed two bags with our clothes and discharged. It seemed downright callous to expect us to put our sopping-wet pants and sweaters and socks back on and walk out into the mid-November chill. But this was a hospital, not a bar, and nobody took up a clothing collection for us. Still wearing our paper gowns, we wincingly pulled on our pants and shoes and Sunny slipped into his life vest (mine had been lost at some point during the rescue) and, slinging the rest of our belongings over our shoulders, we strolled outside. The hospital overlooked the harbor, which now in the late afternoon sun, was restored to the benign vista that sightseers on the Brooklyn Heights Promenade are used to. On Atlantic Avenue, we stood on the curb hailing cabs until one driver, untroubled by the sight of two men wearing hospital gowns and one a life vest, stopped to pick us up and took us back to the bar. No one had even missed us.

It was getting dark but we kept the lights off so as not to be interrupted by a curious passerby. We drank to many things. We drank to Patrolman Louis Balzano—Uncle Gigch—who had always been telling Sunny to take care on the water and who, I now learned, had drowned on duty, like

Ken Hansen, when a pier collapsed beneath him on a spring night in 1950. We drank to Paul Cézanne, whose still lifes had turned out to be life-affirming in a way wholly unexpected, and we drank to ourselves and to the day and to this moment we were having. Sunny was unmistakably pleased by all that had taken place.

"Thank goodness we capsized, Timmy. It would have been mundane if we hadn't tipped over. And thank goodness we're still here to remember all these things!"

15

Ivory-Billed Woodpeckers

THAT SAME WINTER, A STRANGE AND BAROQUE ARTICLE appeared in the local news section of the Sunday newspaper about a man named Joseph Conigliaro who, despite having been shot five times in the face and chest in Red Hook, had driven himself to a hospital only to die on his way into surgery. The story described Conigliaro as an associate of the Gambino crime family who had been in a wheelchair since 1973 after a debt collection went very badly. Conigliaro and a confederate, James Gallo, had spotted a man named Vincent Ensulo, who owed Conigliaro $1600, at a gas station in Red Hook. Seizing the moment, the two men jumped in Ensulo's car, sandwiching him between them, and drove off, each pointing a gun at him. After several blocks, Ensulo took both his destiny and the steering wheel into his hands, and the men opened fire, somehow each missing Ensulo, but not each other. The two went to prison for some years and not too long after they were released they were in trouble again, accused this time of running a loan-sharking business out of a place called John's Luncheonette, described by a district attorney as "a nest of criminal activity on the Brooklyn waterfront."

John's Luncheonette. There was only one business in Red Hook that I knew to be called John's and that was Sunny's. The now-forgotten official name of the bar for decades had been John's Bar and Restaurant. "Bar and Restaurant" was not the same as "Luncheonette" and I figured it was probably a coincidence, that the article was referring to some other place named John's that no longer existed. But still—it was a small neighborhood and I did not really know all that much about the day-to-day operations of the bar in the decades prior to when Sunny began running it. What I did know was that in the past there had not just been nests, but entire colonies of criminal activity on the waterfront.

The following Friday, while there was a lull and we stood behind the bar, I said casually, "Sunny, I read a story in the paper this week about a mob guy named Conigliaro in the neighborhood who was shot while sitting in his car here. Even though he got hit a bunch of times, he was still able to drive himself to a hospital before dying."

"Oh?"

"Yeah. It was quite a strange story. But anyway, the article also said that years ago he used to run a loan-sharking business out of a place called John's in Red Hook. You ever heard of him?"

Sunny did not immediately reply and I thought that I may have crossed a line, a boundary of propriety. Sometimes mentioning the mob to Italian-Americans can have the same effect as mentioning Bill Buckner to a Red Sox fan. They would rather not be reminded. After a moment, and several squinty-eyed draws on his cigarette, he merely said, "Timmy, as much as I'd like to give buoyancy to your imagination, no, I never heard of him."

Buoyancy to my imagination. One of our regulars liked to call Sunny "the philosopher king," but I was beginning to think of him as a poet king.

I would later learn that there had indeed been another John's in Red Hook and that Conigliaro had nothing to do with our bar—at least in recent decades—and that was a very good thing. He sounded like a particularly nasty man. Being a paraplegic did not discourage him from doing the dirtiest jobs. At one point, he was said to have invited a drug dealer to the social club he ran in nearby Carroll Gardens— delightfully named the One Over Golf Club—locked the door behind him, wheeled over to the man, and shot him in the head before his colleagues stuffed sawdust in the victim's mouth to finish him off.

Conigliaro had been better known as Joe Pits, though whether this referred to a love of olives or cherries or to his attitude about life I never found out. His killer chose to shoot him on that particular January day because Joe Pits had left the German shepherd that usually accompanied him every-where at home that afternoon. On his way to the hospital, Joe Pits, mortally wounded, took a detour to pick up a friend, unaware that this was the same man who had ordered his hit and who had loaded his killer's gun with the very bullets that were now inside of him.

I had assumed the mob was historical to Red Hook, that the Red Hook that was home to Joey Gallo and the pet lion he displayed to delinquent debtors; the domain of Anthony

"Tough Tony" Anastasio, the labor leader who fastened a fresh white carnation on his lapel every morning; the terrain of men with names like Carmine the Snake and Frankie Shots—that Red Hook was as much of the past as the shipyards. And even now, the story of Joe Pits read like the story of the aftermath. No lions. No carnations. German shepherds and wheelchairs.

Even so, I began reconsidering what exactly it was that some of the customers who came to the bar did for a living. It was not that I was inclined to pry. But when it came to the mob, I had the curiosity of any person who knew the dialogue of *Mean Streets* by heart. With Joe Pits fresh in my mind, I soon realized that there were several prime candidates for membership in the mobster guild. These men stood apart not because of anything they did that would attract attention to themselves—on the contrary, they had the look and bearing of what one might think of as born-and-raised blue-collar Brooklyn guys. They could pass for firemen or members of Local 282. Still I had the quiet but unmistakable sense that it would be reckless to ever cross them. One such man I will call Casey. He had been coming to the bar since the early 1960s when he began working longshore as a sixteen-year-old; he had been permanently excused from school after his mother had a nurse write a note to his principal that stated he was suffering from a case of the nerves. His face was always flushed as if he was enraged and he was brawny like a lineman, but it was his eyes that reminded me of Mike Ditka—they had the same frank, cutting expression that indicated a low tolerance for fools. A scorpion medallion hung from his neck. His hands were two hammers. He was easily the most intimidating person whom I would ever see in the bar and yet he often appeared to be near tears—especially when he was speaking privately with Sunny. Casey was devoted to Sunny and to Sunny's and once testified to that devotion by saying, "I've fucked hundreds of women but there's no woman's bed I would rather sleep in than sleep on the floor of this bar." By this I knew that Sunny must have felt a great affection and trust for him as well because I didn't know of anyone Sunny would allow to sleep in the bar.

Occasionally, Casey would arrive with a sidekick named Richie, a dark-haired, taciturn man who might have been handsome once before something or someone broke his nose badly. When they weren't huddled at a spot directly by the door, they oftentimes sat in the back room that Sunny used as his painting studio. He stored not only his canvases and painting supplies there but also the spare beer for the bar. Though the room was open, it was considered off limits to customers and the lights were kept turned off. When Casey and Richie were in there, my restocking trips to the fridge were moments of tense silence during which the two of them would stop whatever conversation they had been having and watch me in the dim light as I stacked beer cartons in my arms. After one such encounter, I returned to the bar and while emptying the cases of beer into the cooler, I impulsively asked Sunny, "Is Casey involved in, you know—what he appears to be involved in?"

He looked at me sharply and said, "Timmy. Don't ask me. I may be dumb but I'm not stupid." This was Sunny's way of telling me without telling me.

Years later, I would read with a sense of recognition about the discovery in an Arkansas swamp of a bird known as an ivory-billed woodpecker. The woodpecker had been thought to be extinct for sixty years. But the new sightings of this bird were so fleeting and inconclusive that no one could say for certain whether they had spotted an actual ivory-billed woodpecker or whether it was a case of mistaken identity. I was now having my own passing encounters, ambiguous enough to leave me wondering, *Is he or isn't he? Did I hear correctly . . . ?*

One evening, as I served Budweisers to two men I had never seen before, I overheard just enough of their conversation to understand they were discussing a third man who went by the name Johnny Keyholes. They were ordinary, outright mild-looking men, but what other society of men besides the mob christens an associate with the name Johnny Keyholes? They left soon afterward, before I could listen in on anything else, but the news that somewhere in Brooklyn there was a man known as Johnny Keyholes made me happy for days. When I reported to a friend what I had overheard, she decided that my mob name would be Timmy Bathtubs—those who knew me well would know that I had been named for my habit of making my phone calls, reading the newspaper, and otherwise occupying myself for several hours each day in the bathtub, and those who knew me in passing could make their own darker assumptions.

Another night, another year. A small crowd came in the door. They were mostly late middle-aged and, in a bar where customers usually wore blue jeans, they were dressed conspicuously formally, as if they were coming from an official function or perhaps an anniversary dinner. The women wore dresses and the men sports coats, ties, and frowns—until they saw Sunny. Then they all lit up. The men took turns hugging him and boisterously slapping his shoulder and introducing him to their spouses and dates before moving to a table and pulling up chairs. Sunny turned to me.

"Timmy, do me a kindness," he said. "I know that we don't usually do this but just this once, why don't you go over there and take their order? And, Timmy, don't let them pay!"

There were about a dozen of them and they shouted out their drinks rapidly.

"Scotch, water, no ice."

"Scotch and soda, rocks."

"Scotch, soda, splash of bitters."

I tried keeping track of the order in my head. When I returned with a tray of drinks and mistakenly put a scotch and soda instead of a scotch and water in front of the youngest and most sullen of the men, he looked up at me. Then he looked at the little bubbles popping in his glass. And then he looked at me again.

"Come on, Spidey. Get it right!" he spat. "This isn't Appalachia."

The rest of the evening, whenever I passed their table, he called out, "Hey, Spidey!" and snickered to himself.

As they filed out later, I said to Sunny, "Who *are* those people? And why did that guy keep calling me Spidey?"

"Spidey? I don't know what that's about, Timmy. They're just over from Smith Street. Some are lawyers for the union, actually. Real nice guys."

Only later did I realize Spider had been the hapless waiter taunted and then gunned down by an irritable Joe Pesci in *Goodfellas*. Wise guys or cinephile lawyers? Like the friends of Johnny Keyholes, I could not be sure.

One reason I could not be sure is because Sunny never told. A man who otherwise elevated the recounting of stories and jokes and remembrances, of "holding forth," to an art form, never talked. He did not betray confidences, he did not tell stories about those who did not want stories of themselves to be told. When it came to his own life, he was unsparingly open. There was no indiscretion, no priapic bout with Viagra, no shortcoming of good sense too embarrassing to relate. But when it came to others, and in particular to wise guys, he observed a code that said: you don't tell stories, you don't say names—and if something has to be said, say no more than necessary while still conveying enough truth to satisfy the questioner and your own conscience.

One afternoon a man and a woman knocked on the door. It was a time of day when the bar was usually closed but Sunny happened to be cleaning the counters and, as he told me later, he let them in. They introduced themselves as FBI agents. Sunny said, "Please, let's sit," and the three slid into a booth. The agents explained they were actually hoping to talk to his brother Frank as a possible witness but perhaps Sunny, as someone from the neighborhood, could be of some help. Without indicating yes or no, Sunny nodded for them to continue. They explained that as a result of many interviews they had reason to believe that Frank had taken part in a card game years ago at a nearby bar—long since gone—and witnessed a man shooting and killing another man after being accused of cheating. Did Sunny know of this incident? Sunny said that he had been away from Red Hook for many years and had only heard things after the fact, but to whatever degree hearsay is truth, yes, he had heard of what had taken place. The agents went on to say that the man they suspected of that card-game shooting might himself have recently been murdered, supposedly for killing a made man without permission. They looked at Sunny inquiringly.

Sunny had a good idea of what had happened to the man. He had a good idea because he hung out with guys that hang out. He knew that the man in question, the man the agents named, was the kind of man who liked to hurt people and had always been that way. This man would brag of committing his first murder when he was fourteen. He would say things like, "I'm going to get myself a big gold chain, the biggest fuckin' chain I can find, and I'm going to sit on a bench in Coffey Park and wait for some nigger to try and rob me and I'm going to blow his fuckin' head off." Sunny knew that the guy was said to be such a loose cannon that not even the mob wanted him.

He also knew, you kill a made guy, you're dead, no matter who you are. He knew because everyone who grew up in Red Hook at the time he had grown up knew that.

He looked at the agents. They had the right guy. They were right in suspecting the man for the card-game shooting and they were right to suspect that he was now dead himself. His brother had been at that card game, he was sure. Frank was his favorite sibling but he had always had a theory about him. Being allowed to curse in front of the family while doing his Hitler impersonations had served to tag him with a reputation of being a bad boy, and he had gone on to befriend many of the tough hitters in the neighborhood. Some had become gangsters and killers and Frank himself had been a bit of a thief for a while. Not the kind that would ever harm anyone intentionally, but if he went to a wedding, he'd walk out with the silverware wrapped in a tablecloth, whistling under his breath like he was Santa. That was his nature. He wouldn't go out and stick somebody up or hit them on the head. There had to be a little distance, like stealing from Con Edison. Eventually, he had stopped spending much time around the bad guys in the neighborhood, though he might have sat in on their card games from time to time.

Sunny felt sympathetic toward the agents. He said, "I don't know how you do what you do. I look at you—you're a lovely woman. Perhaps you're married. And you seem like a nice guy. How do you go out there and witness what people do to each other and not take it home to your families? I've seen it from afar and can't get the images out of my mind, you got to see it straight up front."

"We learn to live with it," the woman replied.

"Well, you have my respect for it," Sunny said. "And as to what it is that you are asking about, I can't speak with any kind of authority because I have no personal knowledge of it, but if you're thinking the way I'm thinking, that is, if there's anything to the idea, 'You spit in the air, it comes back down on you' . . . the guy's dead. Aye?"

The agents smiled. "We believe that to be the case," the man said, returning to his breast pocket a notebook in which he had been writing. Realizing that they had gotten all the information they ever would from Sunny, they stood up and shook his hand in a friendly manner.

"We'll come back," they promised. "When we're not on duty."

Nobody wants to be on duty at Sunny's.

Sunny could come across as circumspect and cagey and truthful all at once because not only did Sunny not talk, he did not listen either. That is, he did not listen when it was unadvisable to listen. And it was most unadvisable to listen when wise guys wanted to tell tales or, worse, unburden their consciences.

When he sensed that a man was on the verge of confiding in him something that, as he would put it, was "unpalatable," Sunny would stop him and say, "Please, I don't want you to say something that you may be sorry that you said. It's better if you don't tell me because if it ever gets out that you did things, I don't want you to have to say to yourself, 'Well, I told Sunny.' I don't want you to ever have any doubt in your mind that I'm your friend and that I'm your friend no matter what you did in your life. I know who and what you are to me. We all do things in our life that we are sorry for tomorrow. So we change."

Where Sunny was concerned, wise guys, I had by now come to understand, were no different from the rest of us who came to the bar. They, too, believed they had a special kinship with him. They wanted to drink with him, they wanted his companionship, they wanted his counsel, they wanted to introduce him to their wives and friends the same way I watched so many people introduce him—to show that they were friends with such a singular person and thereby elevate their own standing in their companions' eyes, as if the glow of his incandescence would emanate from them as well.

One year they even invited him to their Christmas party (yes, apparently the mob has Christmas parties). Sunny made sure not to pay attention where they took him. "I think every Mafioso that lived in Brooklyn was there," he told me afterward, though remaining deliberately vague about the details as was his custom. "I was introduced to so-and-so and shook hands with so-and-so. There was this elderly woman, seventy, seventy-five years old, sitting at my table. And I don't think I will ever forget this because it sticks in my mind. It sticks in my belly. When I was introduced to her, I kissed her on the cheek. After doing that, this woman gave me a lot of attention—the attention a mother might give a son. I had my arm on her shoulder and she would tell me a little joke and I'd giggle and I'd give her a little kiss and after a while this guy came over and said to me in this rasping voice, 'You kiss my mother once more, and I'm going to think you're my father!' I said, 'Fuhgeddaboudit!' I stayed away from his mother!

"There was a balcony in the place and at one pernt, this guy got up and he made a Christmas speech. He said, 'I just want to use this opportunity to thank all of you, my dear friends. And also to welcome our new friends to this very special gathering we do at this time of year. I raise my glass to our brotherhood and our friendship.' We held up our glasses and me, I'm thinking, 'What the fuck am I doing?' "

Sunny never expressed misgivings about these friendships; on the contrary, his sense of fraternity was deep-seated. What mattered to him was not a person's occupation, but his having character as well as being one. He showed these made men respect, though not submission, and gave them attention and friendship not for what they did collectively but for who they were individually to him—something, it occurred to me, they may not have been that used to experiencing.

In time he would continue to loosen but never entirely abandon his code of confidentiality. He might point out spots as we drove through Red Hook, for instance, and say, "That's where so-and-so killed so-and-so."

"Who's so-and-so?" I'd ask.

"He was the brother of what's-his-name."

He never did say names, and he could do this without feeling apologetic about it because he always had made it a point not to know names—or quickly forget them if he did.

The only exception I ever knew him to make was for his friend Blackjack, and then only because he was no longer alive and Sunny felt compelled one night to give a spontaneous eulogy, even if it was only an intimate one in a car outside of a restaurant while he finished a last pre-dinner cigarette. He would often do this, bring up a person, an event, out of the blue, a sign that his mind was in at least two places at once.

"I had this friend once. He wasn't a made guy but he might have been connected only because his brother was a made guy. I really loved him. I won't say his full name but his nickname was Blackjack. I never called him that. I called him by his first name, Frankie. He was famous for using a blackjack whenever there was some kind of trouble. Frankie, he had a great sense of humor and nothing he would say didn't have something that wasn't humorous in it. He talked really rough, like, 'I'll cut that fuckin' guy's balls off! I'm gonna get that son of a bitch.' He looked a little like Al Pacino. I actually don't really like Al Pacino because I always get this feeling he's playing my friend Frankie. It always sounds to me like he's trying to copy him but never quite making it. Frankie was the real deal, but this other guy, Al Pacino . . . Frankie, if he had been an actor, he would have played himself. It was like that, aye?

"Frankie loved clothes. He would sometimes show up at the bar like he was going to play golf. A golf suit, a colorful hat. He was always impeccable, even when he was hurting. He had diabetes and after they cut his toes off, he was supposed to use a wheelchair but he had too much dignity for that. So he would use a little cane and every day he would get out. He had one seat that he always sat in. The last booth, closest to the terlet. He wasn't supposed to smoke but smoking to him was an art. Frankie would sit down and put his ashtray here, he'd put his cigarettes here, and he'd put his beer over here. And a napkin. All in a row. As rough and as gruff as he was, he was so fuckin' neat, aye? So beautifully put together. Everything had a place and everything was in its place. You never went up to his table and said, 'Frankie, can I have a cigarette?' and grabbed it. You would never do that because you respected him so much and you didn't want to disrupt his style of life. And you didn't just go sit next to him either. You'd say, 'Frankie, may I sit?' In doing these things, you didn't feel like you were being humbled or your sense of pride and dignity were being diminished. You did them simply because he would do the same for you.

"Well, when we started getting a little busier here at the bar, and by busy, I mean two dozen people, I said to Frankie one night, 'I can't handle this by myself. I need your help.' He said, 'Sunny, I can't work behind the bar. I got to hobble. It'll take me ten minutes to get from here to there.' So I said to him, 'Why don't you just hang out up by the front of the bar, greet people, take their orders, and I'll do the running around?'

"He went home, took a shower, shaved, came in wearing a pressed white shirt, and he did a beautiful job, aye? We continued for several weeks like this.

"So what happened, at some pernt, some of the people coming in . . . well, some might have been gay, some not, but they had an educated manner. If you didn't speak a certain way, if you had a little bit of something sissified about you, you were in trouble with Frankie. Which is why it always got me that he befriended me because I'm not what you would consider a typical Brooklyn guy, you know?

"Anyway, on one particular night, Frankie and Casey, who was a good friend of his, were here and the place started filling up with what he called 'the fuckin' ricchioni.' That's Italian slang for, 'Here come the faggots.' He embarrassed somebody and so I said to him, 'Frankie, if anyone here is a ricchione, the biggest ricchione is me!' Now, Frankie's respect for me was such that when I said that to him, he felt he might have offended me because now he was uncertain as to what my persuasion was. And after he went home a little while later, Casey came to me and said, 'Sunny, I have never, never heard somebody speak back to Frankie the way you did. And by you saying what you said, you turned him around in such a way, he's never going to call somebody a faggot or a ricchione again, because of his respect for you.' I could tell by this that Casey wasn't certain as to what my persuasion was either so I said, 'Casey, I had to say that because in what other way am I going to be communicable enough, tactful enough, diplomatic enough? I can't tell him, "Leave the fags alone." I know that he loves me and if he thinks of me before he says something like that, he's not going to say it.'

"Frankie, he was a sweet guy. When he was in the hospital not too long before he died, Casey and I went and visited with him. And Casey, he cried."

16

Two Roses

Somewhere in the National Archives there is a service record for one Airman Antonio Raffaele Balzano. I suspect it's as deeply buried as that of Beetle Bailey, who enlisted in the army the year before him. Sunny may have been, by his own design, the most inept serviceman in all the branches of the military. That he ever served at all was an implausibility on par with the military careers of Private James M. Hendrix, 101st Airborne, and Staff Sergeant Leonard S. Nimoy. After all, the Sunny I knew was something of a latter-day Oscar Wilde—the embodiment of freethinking individualism and compliance to no other authority than one's own conscience. The only movements in which he was a believer were Cubism and Abstract Expressionism. Whatever customs, discipline, or ideology the United States Air Force might have imprinted upon him, none of it remained.

Though it was the height of the Korean War, it was a sex-

ual rather than a patriotic fervor that prompted Sunny to en-
list in the first place. As a teenager, he attended George
Westinghouse, a trade high school in downtown Brooklyn,
where he studied silver- and gold-smithing while also ap-
prenticing to a jeweler in lower Manhattan. In the afternoons,
he boxed with the Red Hook Police Athletic League, where
his stablemates shared their green-and-white shorts and their
crabs. He was undecided whether he wanted to become a
boxing jeweler or a jewelry-making boxer when he was surprised one day by his best friend, George Hunt, who showed
up at his school. "I'm going to sign up for the Air Force and
serve for four years instead of waiting to get drafted into the
army for two and being sent to Korea and fuckin' dying," he
had said. "Why don't you come with me? If we're lucky, we
might get sent to Italy or Germany. Or the South Pacific.
We'll see the world together—or at least something else.
You'll lose your virginity to a Fräulein with big tits or to
whatever they call the women in Okinawa. Anyway, we'll
get the fuck out of Red Hook, that's for sure."

Sunny had never given the idea of enlisting any thought
before but he had given his virginity the near-constant con-
sideration of any seventeen-year-old. George was a couple
years older and he always seemed to know his vulnerabilities.

Sunny was not of enlistment age and needed a parent's
consent, so he had gone to his father. "I don't want you to
go," his father had said. "You're my oldest son. I always hoped
you would stay and help Uncle John and me run the bar. And
in time, it would be yours. Not Uncle John's bar. Not Ralph's
bar. Sunny's."

By then Sunny had begun to hate the bar. When he had

been younger, he had often come in after school for his lunch and his father used to put his arm around his shoulders and introduce him to customers by saying, "This is my thoroughbred." Sunny hadn't been sure what that meant, only that it made him feel good about himself. His father always seemed to have that ability. But after his uncle John returned from fighting in France, Sunny began avoiding the bar. Gloomy and ill-tempered, John was the type of man to whom one never wanted to express one's hopes or enthusiasms. If he displayed any affection toward a customer, it probably meant he didn't like him. He never complimented Sunny and more typically said things that made him want to crawl into a corner. Once, Sunny walked in with a new dream in his head and announced to his father that he would like to become an actor. His uncle gazed over the bar at him and sneered, "Who do you think you are? Paul Muni?" He was a joy killer.

So in response to his father's pleas to stay, Sunny said, "Dad, I can't do that. I don't want to stay in the neighborhood and I don't want to end up like you." Right away he felt sorry he'd said it that way but his father just replied, "This is not something I want you to do, but if your heart is set on it, I'll sign the paper."

The recruiter had promised that if Sunny and George enlisted together they would serve their tours of duty together, but the day of their induction was the last Sunny spent with George Hunt. Subsequently, of the world he saw Plattsburgh, New York; Amarillo, Texas; and Riverside, California. There were no Fräuleins, only a two-day leave with other enlistees to a brothel in Tijuana where he found himself in a dimly lit, cavernous room humping a woman on a well-worn cot several feet away from another airman humping on a cot who was several feet from the next airman humping—and so on down the line. Apparently in the military, even this was done in formation.

He had thought that his jeweler's knowledge of the properties of metals might qualify him to become a metallurgist. But instead he had been sent to aircraft mechanics school in Texas before being stationed at March Air Force Base in the San Bernardino Valley. His last illusions of becoming a prize-fighter had been beaten out of him in basic training by a heavier man goaded into a homicidal mood by the commanding officers. He knew he had made a great mistake and that he was entirely unsuited to the military and to being a mechanic. The sergeants reminded him of the spiteful nuns in school, and the noise, the oil, the smell of kerosene reminded him of things he'd hated in Red Hook. Not long after his arrival in California he plotted his own general discharge. He decided that in the course of the next spot inspection by the maintenance crew chiefs, during which mechanics were quizzed about various operations of the aircraft, he would respond with blatantly stupid answers. Of course he knew the correct terminology and right answers—he would have to work at being stupid. Brooklyn stupid.

When the day of the inspection had come, an officer led him over to the back of one of the six jet engines on his aircraft, the B-47 Stratojet, and pointed to a component and asked, "Can you name these particular parts of the aircraft and describe what degree of importance they have?" The officer was expecting to hear, "Those are discharge thermocouples that measure the exhaust temperature and send a voltage reading to the exhaust gas temperature gauge located on the right side of the pilot's instrument panel," but instead Sunny replied, "Oh, dees things? Dey're like candles. Dey get hot and dey're wired to de area where de pilot sits and what dey do is dey tell de pilot and de navigator how much heat is comin' out of dis part of de airplane." The inspector recorded everything Sunny said on a clipboard. Then he pointed to a hydraulic accumulator and asked him to explain its function. Sunny knew that the accumulators stored pressure that is always kept at a constant in order to hydraulically move sections of the bomber such as the nose wheel, the wing flaps, the windshield wipers. So he explained, "Dis is like a balloon. It holds de air and when de men who sit in de cockpit want to turn de airplane, dey press a button on der instrument panel and it releases de air from de balloon."

Sunny was ordered out of the hangar on the spot.

For a period of time, Sunny became the company artist, illustrating aircraft maintenance tips for its monthly bulletin. He felt his natural abilities were finally being recognized, but this period of relative contentment only lasted until the next wing redeployment when Sunny, left behind, was appointed squadron gardener. He carefully mowed the flower beds and pruned the lawns and decimated the roses that ringed the officers' quarters, but no one seemed to notice his horticultural ineptitude. Undaunted, he developed a case of phantom back pain. At the sick bay he punched the air, howled, and wept until his superiors capitulated. He was relieved of his gardening duties and assigned to the military police, though not the branch that wore uniforms and carried sidearms and did actual policing. Instead, he was delivered every night to guard duty on the flight line, so far from all activity that took place on the base that it felt like he was being sent into overnight exile.

He hadn't ever known such cold. Growing up, his home had often seemed like the coldest address in New York. Where there was a breeze elsewhere in Brooklyn, there was a bluster in Red Hook and an all-out gale on his block. Closing the front door was often a minor battle. But here, the cold not only got into one's boots, one's feet, one's chest, but into one's thoughts. It was the cold of the desert in winter, the cold of the stars, but also the cold of being alone in the dark on a deserted tarmac. He didn't remember ever feeling so forlorn and forgotten and out of place in his life.

There were other men like him out in the dark, assigned to guard duty on the far end of the flight line, each separated from the next by a row of aircraft. He assumed they all did as he did—curl up on the ground soon after the taillights of the truck that delivered them to these remote runways disappeared, half-sleeping and half-listening for the hum of the hourly patrol jeep ferrying the sergeant-in-charge and sometimes hot coffee around the airfield. Occasionally a fire engine would make a training run up and down the runway. The nights could get tremendously foggy in this part of Southern California and on one such night a fire truck ran over the head of one of the guards. After that, Sunny had begun lying directly underneath the planes. In their bellies hung nuclear bombs meant for targets across the Pacific Ocean, and he sometimes felt a momentary wonder at his proximity to objects of such power and purpose; other times they only served to remind him of his own impotence and aimlessness. When he slept he often dreamt of home but also of detonations in distant places. When he awoke intermittently he would concentrate to hear something, anything, but usually he heard nothing. No crickets, no birds, no Soviet agents, no Korean saboteurs. He would tuck his chin into his jacket and close his eyes again, though the sheer stillness would keep him from falling into any kind of deeper sleep. Often he would go over in his mind the turns of fate that had brought him to this unhappy place. He thought of his mother and father, of George Hunt, of girls.

One night he thought of another night.

He had been brought to a bar, several blocks up Conover Street from his family's place, by his friend Nicky Rose. Nicky was older and of drinking age. The only other people there were the Irish owner, Joe; his bartender; and a girl whose name also happened to be Rose. Just Rose. Nicky wasn't quite a criminal but he had ambitions of being one, and in the past Sunny had accompanied him as he ran small errands for the oldest of the Gallo brothers. The bar owner had never done a good deed in his life as far as Sunny knew. He was the kind of person who would never challenge anyone if he had any doubt he could beat them. The bartender was even worse. Both men hurt people and didn't have a conscience about it. And then there was Rose. She was slow, and it was said that she would sleep with anyone. What this really meant was she would sleep with the navy sailors and merchant marines who were in port. Servicemen and seamen were usually so hard up, they had few compunctions about having sex with someone who was trusting and slow of mind. Sunny would have been glad to be anywhere else at that moment, but he was in a stage of his life where he still deferred to people who were his elders, even if by only a few years. Nicky wanted to be in good standing with Joe and Sunny wanted to be in good standing with Nicky, so they were all together that night.

A sailor came in, from where no one knew. He sat at the bar and after he had a few drinks, he said to no one in particular, "I'd really like to suck her cunt."

Nothing was said and the man looked up at the bartender. "I said, I'd really like to suck her cunt. Maybe you can set something up for me? I'll pay."

He pulled out a roll of bills.

"Anyone who would suck that woman's cunt would eat shit," the bartender replied, loud enough for everyone to hear. Sunny knew that he and Joe would have Rose do whatever they wanted when they were alone. The bartender walked over to where Joe was sitting and Joe muttered, "Let's jump this guy." The barkeep gave him a nod and Joe turned to Nicky and Sunny, who were leaning on the bar, and said under his breath, "Nicky, you two go out the side door. We're going to put this guy out. When he walks through that door, you're going to grab him and I'm going to slug him. Understand?"

It all happened very quickly and as Joe had said it would. Sunny followed Nicky outside, uncertain as to what was about to take place. He hadn't had time to consider the possibilities. It was dark and the side of the building they had emerged from was hidden from the view of passersby. When the sailor came moments later, Nicky seized him from the front by both arms.

Clunk!

"Ugghh."

"Je-SUS!"

The sailor sank to the pavement. Joe stood in the doorway, holding a monkey wrench. Sunny looked down at the man, now laid out in front of him. He was spellbound and disbelieving. The blow had been hard, as if Joe had put all his weight into it. The two men were now on top of the sailor and going through his pockets.

"Come on, Sunny. Let's get the fuck out of here!"

Nicky and Sunny ran down Conover Street, past his father's bar and down to the pier at the end of the street. They sat on the edge of a dock and looked across the water. Sunny felt sick to his stomach. He felt like mud. He felt like the sound the wrench made when it hit the sailor's head.

The next day, Nicky saw Sunny on the street and handed him twenty dollars and said, "Here's your half."

"What happened to . . . ?"

"The fuck do I know. We don't want to know, you know?"

Sunny took the money. He didn't hear anything in the neighborhood about it that day or the next. He didn't see the police around that bar. He never learned what happened to the sailor. Nicky didn't talk about it. Sunny didn't talk about it. He knew he didn't have anything to do with it in any real sense, but lying in the dark in Southern California he could still hear the sound of the wrench hitting the man's skull. It had been as powerful as if they had shot bullets into him. He didn't know, he would never know, if the sailor had managed to get up and go to his ship or if he had been dragged off and killed.

When he thought about it, he supposed Nicky Rose was still in Red Hook, trying to get the attention of the Gallo brothers, and Slow Rose was probably still going off with men who paid her a compliment. To his surprise, Sunny felt something like gratitude at that moment. Things could have turned out worse for him—his life might not have changed at all. And when he heard the rumble of an approaching jeep and saw its tapered sweep of light on the runway, he got up and stood at attention.

17

Samsara

When I heard the learn'd astronomer;
When the proofs, the figures, were ranged in columns
*   before me;*
When I was shown the charts and the diagrams, to add,
*   divide, and measure them;*
When I, sitting, heard the astronomer, where he
*   lectured with much applause in the lecture-room,*
How soon, unaccountable, I became tired and sick;
Till rising and gliding out, I wander'd off by myself,
In the mystical moist night-air, and from time to time,
Look'd up in perfect silence at the stars.

—WALT WHITMAN, 1865

"When Uncle John was alive, I would come by late in
the afternoon to read the newspapers and the bar would
be entirely empty. There wouldn't be a sound in the

place. Uncle John allowed himself one single bottle of beer a day and he would open that bottle and open my bottle and we would sit together on the stoop if it was warm or inside in a booth. Some days the light from the setting sun would come through the window and illuminate the whole front area of the bar in this great orange glow and one could see, floating in this light, millions and millions of specks of dust and we would watch this universe of dust rise and fall in silence until we finished our beers and I would wish him good night."

—JOHN, *private investigator, at Sunny's, late 1990s*

18

Two Joes

A
FTER A NEWSPAPER REPORTER CAME TO THE BAR
once to interview Sunny for a profile he planned to
write for *The New York Times,* a few customers were dis-
turbed enough by what they considered the possibility of un-
desirable attention for the bar that they talked of leaving
threatening messages at the man's office to dissuade him from
filing his story. I suggested a more sinister approach—sending
a card blank but for a black hand.

The truth was that by now, any hope of keeping the existence of Sunny's quiet had evaporated. Though Red Hook
was still largely unvisited by the late 1990s, great crowds had
begun to fill the bar on Friday nights, bringing to mind a
Mardi Gras procession that had taken a wrong turn into a
blind alley—the early arrivals were wedged tighter and
tighter, mostly without protest, while the rear continued to
file in without letup. People came on foot, by bicycle, boat,
car, and cab, oftentimes gleefully recounting their fretful

driver's initial refusal to drive to Red Hook and the many wrong turns it had taken before they'd finally arrived here. One woman was momentarily spooked when her driver stopped his taxi on a shadowy street and got out of the car, but was soon relieved to see him kneel down to read a map in the light of his headlamp.

It gave some an evident thrill to travel to Red Hook, an idea which amused several of the natives at the bar a good deal and who alternately referred to the new arrivals as pilgrims—if they were women—or pussies—if they were men. They did this out of earshot of Sunny. He found few things more annoying than a Sunny's regular who acted as if he were a founding member of an exclusive club.

As the number of customers swelled, Sunny enlisted the help of a local woman named Isaura, known as Izzy, whose single qualification to be a bartender, according to Sunny, was that "she's a natural." What this meant was that she possessed a God-given geniality and a deep-rooted mothering instinct, something for which there is a greater need in most bars than the ability to make a Black Russian. Izzy had raised two children in Red Hook as well as several animals, including a vagrant cat found wandering the street with a stick protruding from its rectum. As Sunny opined, if she knew what to do with a cat in such straits, she would know how to handle a customer who only acted as though he had a stick up his ass.

The only other adaptations that Sunny made were first opening up the back room, previously solely used for placing phone calls, and eventually surrendering his painting studio in the rear of the building, giving the expanded bar the layout of a shotgun house. When someone wondered aloud why Sunny didn't simply open on other nights to disperse the concentration of people, he said that doing so would "take away the speciality of it."

While the nights still began and ended with periods of near-total stillness, the hours in between teetered between bedlam, bliss, elation, and excess. At their height, people spanned the length and width of all three rooms and drinks were handed back bucket-brigade style. A bagpiper, who played police and fireman funerals by day, would sometimes suddenly erupt. A surer method of crowd dispersal I have yet to see.

Although there was a good deal of country and western as well as soul music, including the Memphis sound, the Chicago sound, the New Orleans sound, and, occasionally, the Philadelphia sound, the prevailing songs on the stereo were usually of the Top 10 variety ... from the heyday of the League of Nations. On any given night, one might hear the Ink Spots, the Mills Brothers, Slim & Slam, the Texas Playboys, both Dorseys, Ukulele Ike, Harlan Lattimore, Chick Bullock, Krupa, Noble, Whiteman, Beiderbecke, Armstrong, Trumbauer, Holiday, as well as the twentieth century's noblest peerage: Count Basie, Duke Ellington, and Kings Oliver and Cole.

By tradition, live music still began around ten o'clock. A corner of the room near the front door served as the unofficial bandstand and one often had to shimmy around a guitar or fiddle bow in order to enter or leave. Most of the acts belonged either to the honky-tonk or the Texas roadhouse school. The most soulful of these was a country blues revivalist named John Pinamonti. The most consummately ramshackle was a trio who called themselves the Gowanus Canal Boys, and when they started up with "Sea of Heartbreak" or

"Pick Me Up on Your Way Down" or "Cold, Cold Heart" or any other song whose theme was despair, despondency, or defeatism, waves of euphoria would sweep through the room. An amateur zoologist said that the sight of these moments reminded him of the phenomenon of flocking in the natural world—when schools of fish or large congregations of birds such as starlings or pigeons all turn and swoop in unison, their backs and undersides flashing light and dark, maneuvers so synchronized that the flock appears to be acting as one organism sending a Morse code to the universe.

THERE WERE A great number of eccentrics at Sunny's during this period. They were of both the deliberate and the unaffected variety. Some were regulars and some were only passing through. A hurdy-gurdy player who sat on a bench and cranked out medieval melodies until he was begged to stop. A bug eater from Coney Island named Insectavora (she left hungry). One transvestite appeared on an enormous tricycle in the summer and sang "Lydia the Tattooed Lady." Another came to a Christmas fish fry and sang "The Girl From Ipanema." When I once remarked to Sunny that neither had ever returned, he said, "Thank goodness they never came back! Their beauty was their rarity."

Some of these new customers would become great friends of mine, including a moon-eyed nurse who invariably cried at the mention of mothers, miners, or Mets—she loved the first two and assisted the surgeons operating on the third. Musicians were quietly asked not to play Merle Travis's "Dark as a Dungeon" when she was present to avoid the sudden onset of tears. In her spare time she collected both the head and pubic hair of friends and strangers, the talons and wings of dead birds she came across, and prosthetic glass eyes, assembling them into dolls that contravened the laws of nature and in some cases, decency. Mercifully, vivification was beyond her abilities. At some point she thought she might have some use for the lint that had built up around the edge of an industrial fan, and proceeded to mangle a finger. On Halloween, she liked to dress up the remaining nub, say as a pirate or, on the eve of the Kentucky Derby, as a jockey. Her future husband had a great interest in birds and he arrived at the bar on occasion wearing a hat made from a deceased Canada goose he had found alongside an Illinois road. The hat's wingspan was wider than the bar door; he entered sideways. When they decided to marry, they traveled to Madagascar, onetime home of the world's largest bird, the aepyornis, to see its skeleton in person and to wed themselves beneath the entwined trunks of two baobab trees known as the Baobab Amoureux. The bride wore nothing but red the entire three-week trip. Red is the color of passion.

There was a twosome who by day painted themselves metallic silver and stood as inanimate as out-of-service robots on Manhattan streets and subway platforms; they called themselves the Mercury Men but at the bar they were known, to some of the wags if not to themselves, as the Harvard Boys, for their love of argyle socks and horn-rimmed glasses when not on duty.

The more down-to-earth eccentrics were those who, like Sunny, were unaware that there was anything particularly unusual about them in any way.

There was the neighborhood firebrand, John McGettrick, possessor of the knee-length mustache. After part had frozen

and broken off one cold night, his wife had had him trim the
other side. "For symmetry," he explained matter-of-factly.
He could often be found talking to a pigtailed, bearded glass-
blower named Pete, who had once lived on a restored Hudson riverboat moored at the end of the street before moving
into a tar-paper house without plumbing around the corner.
Pete weighed in the vicinity of three hundred pounds, which
wouldn't have been notable if his paternal grandparents had
not both been members of the sideshow troupe Rose's Royal
Midgets. He was nearly always in the company of a small
black dog named Shadow when he came to Sunny's; the two
liked to sit at the bar together, sharing fellowship and, I suspected, Wild Turkey.

One of my favorite customers was Joe. Middle-aged, with
coal-black eyes beneath coal-black hair, Joe customarily sat
on the barstool the farthest into the bar, a corner where his
back was to a wall and from which he could survey the entire
room while smoking cigars. Joe claimed that seat was one of
his three treasured places on earth—the other two were the
ancient Black Hills of South Dakota where he had vacationed
one summer (he had an interest in all things Native American) and the newly opened Bellagio hotel in Las Vegas. He
was of Sicilian and, by his telling, gangster lineage and although he owned a successful freight transportation business
in Manhattan, Joe did little to discourage the assumption that
he was both made and self-made. He drove a pricey car,
smoked pricey tobacco, and took himself out to eat at pricey
restaurants nearly every night. He did not like to be photo-
graphed and made it a point to turn his head away whenever
someone was about to snap a picture elsewhere in the bar.
Each Friday, Joe reached into his sport-coat pocket and

handed each of us behind the bar an unblemished fifty- or hundred-dollar bill whose provenance I did not question. He seemed genuinely moved when I returned from a vacation in the Southwest with a present for him—a silver Navajo money clip that I had decided best combined two of his great passions.

Joe would sometimes tell me that one of the reasons he liked coming to Sunny's was because he imagined that his grandfather had sat on these same barstools and looked at his reflection in the same bar mirror when he was a young man. He maintained that the ruthless Johnny Friendly in *On the Waterfront* was based not on Albert Anastasia as is generally assumed, but on his own grandfather, a waterfront boss who, he said, had dispatched several of his rivals personally.

Joe's true peculiarity was in his exceedingly mannerly behavior. In an uncourtly age, good manners can seem eccentric.

He firmly believed that an unaccompanied woman should never pay for her own drink and if he spotted one approaching the bar to order, he would call out to the nearest bartender that he would be taking care of it. He was motivated by an intuitive chivalry; this is how a gentleman behaved in the past and ought to behave today and tomorrow. Inevitably and anonymously, he also bought everyone sitting at the bar a round once, and often twice, a night, in these instances prompted by a Catholic sense of charity and by the predicament of simply having too much cash. (He confided to me that he was always looking for ways to shed some of his paper holdings.) He would continue his generous practices for the many years he would spend at the bar until he had the misfortune of buying a drink for one of the place's most prominent temptresses. Even Sunny knew to keep some distance from her. Joe's probity was no match against her considerable charms and this passing weakness must have shamed him greatly, because after the affair ran its course, he never returned again.

NOT TOO LONG after I had met Sunny, I took the subway to the Upper West Side for the memorial service of the famous *New Yorker* writer Joseph Mitchell. One of the features of living in New York was that while one may not be able to meet many of its illustrious figures in life, one could often go to their funerals. In recent years, I had been to Cab Calloway's and Dizzy Gillespie's. After I got home from Mitchell's memorial that night, I reread some of his essays, including his famous barography of McSorley's Ale House in which a man recalls the customers of a tavern in his native Ireland: "I enjoyed observing them and I enjoyed listening to them. They were like actors in a play, only the play was real. There were Falstaffs among them—that is, they were just windy old drunks from the back alleys of Ballyragget, but they were Falstaffs to me. And there were Ancient Pistols among them. . . . There were good old souls among those men, and there were leeches among them."

I would think of that passage many times. It was wonderfully apt of Sunny's, not because everyone behaved in the exaggerated manner of a stage actor, though there was a Falstaff at Sunny's as well—a burly, bug-eyed tilesetter who, instead of making a low-key entrance like any ordinary customer, preferred to barge in as if escaping a downpour, gruffly shout, "Sunny, you old faggot!," hand him a bouquet of flowers, and proceed to stare down anyone who met his eyes. Rather, it was that Fridays would bring a procession of disparate personalities into the bar unlike one I found anywhere else. Some behaved extraordinarily. Very few were dull.

Joseph Mitchell famously wrote his last story for *The New Yorker* in 1964, and for the following thirty-some years, went to work every day, closed his office door behind him, and never published another word. I know little else about him, but I know that meeting Sunny and coming to his bar would have reminded him of some of the things he loved in life.

19

Kennedy

SUNNY RARELY STRAYED VERY FAR FROM RED HOOK OF his own accord. Our near-catastrophic expedition to Jurassic Park had served to further persuade him to keep close to home and let the world come to him at the bar. He hadn't lost his sense of inquisitiveness, in particular for art and theater, but as sociable as he was with customers on Fridays, Sunny was somewhat of a reclusive man the rest of the week. "I'm good company to myself," he would say. He largely avoided his family, explaining, "I love 'em but I don't like 'em." He enjoyed people but rarely crowds, nature only if he could observe it from his window or while smoking a cigarette on his roof. He greeted Tone's suggestions that they drive to Prospect Park and take a walk as he might the proposal that one pay a visit to a proctologist just to pass the time. Smoking in bed, he watched television with the avidity of Chauncey Gardiner, preferring old movies starring William Bendix or Marlon Brando. One of his most treasured possessions, a gift from an actor, was a ring that had once belonged to Brando and which he would slip on when *Sayonara* or *Streetcar* or *The Godfather* was showing.

For a period of time, to his surprise, he received what he called "the bunny channel," which he would watch when he was sure he was alone in the house, making a well-rehearsed switch to the History Channel when he heard Tone's footsteps approaching in the hallway.

He could lose himself for hours sketching in notebooks or working on his multilayered, highly colorful paintings. He kept a translucent glass brick next to his painting supplies, and like the drunkard philosopher who claims he can think clearest when his mind is cloudiest, Sunny would occasionally hold the brick up to his eyes to help him see lines less linearly.

On the occasions that he did leave the neighborhood, it was usually someone else's idea. After a few more outings, I began to see why. Without any effort on his part, Sunny always drew attention to himself. For starters, there was his appearance. Sunny could often look highly disheveled. He wore his hair in the style of a castaway and if he went several days without shaving, he began to look like a castaway who has given up hope of seeing civilization again. He was underweight and his clothes hung loosely on his frame and were usually of a mismatched combination. If he was feeling natty, he would put on a creaseless white dress shirt and tuck it in the waistband of his mail-order sweatpants. He had an acute fear of feeling cold and if he was invited to go out to a restaurant in the wintertime, he liked to wear a sky-blue one-piece insulated ski suit beneath a dark blazer. After Tone gave him a pair of felt house slippers one year, he stopped wearing any other kind of shoe. On one excursion, to the Metropolitan Museum of Art, I looked at his pants with suspicion while we were standing in the lobby.

"You're wearing long underwear."

"Oh?" he replied. "I guess my underwear is my outerwear today!"

No one ever seemed to forget meeting Sunny, no matter how briefly, and over the years all of these introductions had kept accruing to the point that Sunny, through no other agent than the force of his personality, had become one of the more famous figures in Brooklyn, and apparently several of the other boroughs. He once admitted that even when he had run out of essential groceries, he hesitated to go to the store because by the time he reached the cash register, he had been stopped and greeted by so many well-wishers that the experience would wear him out. He deemed Staten Island to be the most desirable locale to have dinner out solely because it was the place in which he was least likely to be accosted.

Even when he wasn't recognized, he possessed the kind of face that caused people to do double takes and stare after him as if asking themselves, "Where have I seen that man before?" Two of the last living nuns in Red Hook, Sisters Dorothy and Olivia, were so taken by his resemblance to the son of God, when they bumped into him one day, that they asked him whether he would consider the lead in a performance of the Stations of the Cross at their Easter pageant. He had been cast as King Duncan in the Brooklyn Stage Company's production of *Macbeth* several years earlier, a role he had taken to with such zeal that people were still talking about Sunny frothing at the mouth as one of the greatest examples of method acting they had ever seen. He happily agreed to the nuns' request and his performance was so convincing that one of the sisters later exclaimed, "We actually crucified Sunny!" They asked him to reprise his role the following year in a double bill of *The Woman at the Well* and *The Woman Taken in Adultery* and for a time afterward, some of the more devout older ladies in Red Hook would cross themselves when passing him on the street.

THE ONLY OTHER person that I had known who possessed a similar charisma to Sunny's was my first employer in New York: George Plimpton. Like Sunny, he both stood a head taller than most people and had such a distinctive bearing and manner that in a crowd, one's eyes would fall on him first and naturally. The description of him I always found to be the most accurate was his own: "I am built rather like a bird of the stilt-like, wader variety—the avocets, the limpkins, and herons," he wrote in *Shadow Box,* his greatest book. This implied both a stick-figure physique, which he had, and also a willowy grace and unflinching steadiness. Glimpsing George Plimpton at a museum opening or in the stands at a game or in a crowd waiting for the light to change at York Avenue was like seeing a regal snowy egret standing amidst a gathering of pigeons.

Plimpton was most at ease with people younger than himself, which probably accounted for the enduring friendship we had maintained over the years since we met. I had invited him to Sunny's on several occasions, even though the idea of George Plimpton, as confirmed an Upper East Sider as one might be, hanging out in Red Hook, let alone Brooklyn, was as far-fetched as spotting Tom Wolfe working out at

Gleason's Gym. It just wasn't his habitat. But I was convinced that Plimpton would be drawn to Sunny in much the way he was drawn to Muhammad Ali and Marianne Moore—that he would recognize a person who is so effortlessly articulate and frequently lyrical that one regrets one cannot memorize every conversation one has with him. After all, Plimpton was one of these people himself. One afternoon I was playing pool with him in his living room and after I had smacked the cue ball into the rack with particular violence, he exclaimed admiringly, "That sounded like a covey of partridges exploding!"

A few years into my sojourn at Sunny's, Plimpton invited me to his midtown men's club for a game of court tennis—an obscure sport that he had mastered and that I had never played—and as we stood in our neighboring changing cubicles afterward, he mentioned that he would be coming to Brooklyn, to emcee a Moth storytellers event at the Brooklyn Academy of Music, and he thought that I might like to come.

Since I knew of no better storyteller than Sunny and simply because his company made just about any excursion far more unpredictable than it would have been without him, I invited Sunny to join me.

I wasn't sure whether the name George Plimpton would mean anything to Sunny. When it came to popular culture, I was often surprised at what he did and did not know. Certainly, he had heard of the Beatles, but he would be hard-pressed to name any of their songs. He considered Jimmy Durante to be a major historical figure, nearly as prominent as Popeye, but he might have trouble naming the president who came between Nixon and Carter. However, when I told him in the car over that Plimpton was to be the host of the evening, he let out a small cry.

"George Plimpton!" he exclaimed. "Wow. Timmy, I feel that I've been following George Plimpton as far back as the beginning of television. He was there in the early days of Jackie Gleason and Jack Benny. I believe he had a talk show even before Steve Allen, who is considered the original talk show host. He has a way about him that is so unique. Although his manner of speech is sophisticated, he has always seemed like a humble man who has very common tastes. Such as boxing. That is probably why I have always liked him so much."

I happened to know that Plimpton's first appearance on any type of screen wasn't until 1962, when he played a Bedouin in *Lawrence of Arabia* (as fanciful a casting choice as there ever has been), but Sunny's mythologizing of Plimpton was, as usual, more entertaining than the petty facts and I didn't correct him. Instead, I went on to tell him how I had come to work for Plimpton when I first moved to New York and that of all of his storied exploits, I considered his stint as the triangle player with the New York Philharmonic and his three-round fight with light-heavyweight Archie Moore to be my favorites. When I told him that in Plimpton's bathroom hung a ring robe with the faded letters "Muhammad Ali" spelled out on the back, Sunny's eyes widened.

"My goodness," he said. "Muhammad Ali. If I were to put on Jesus's cloak, it certainly would do something for me. But Ali's robe . . . I tell you what, if I could put on Muhammad Ali's robe while wearing my Marlon Brando ring, the alchemy would be such—fuhgeddaboudit!"

When we arrived at BAM, Plimpton was standing off to

himself as people filed in, studying a notebook and appearing oddly forlorn. I called out to him and he looked up with genuine relief.

"George, meet Sunny."

Sunny took hold of Plimpton's hand with great vigor and said, "George. May I say I have followed you for many years and for all that it is that it is that you do, you have my greatest admiration and respect. Welcome home, George!"

Plimpton appeared simultaneously bewildered and delighted by this reception. He couldn't have known that Sunny routinely greeted people as though they were prodigal sons of Brooklyn.

I might have introduced Sunny as a saloon owner, painter, actor, or in any number of ways but instead I said, "You two have something in common, George. You both spent time in the ring. I was telling Sunny on our way over here how Archie Moore once broke your nose and how Muhammad Ali's robe hangs in your bathroom."

"Ali, yes," Plimpton said, in his typical oratorical fashion. "For some reason I never fully understood, he always called me Kennedy. Like the president. He must have detected a similarity in our manner or our speech."

"Sunny was at one time a fighter as well as the proprietor of his own boxing club in Red Hook."

Sunny beamed.

"Oh?" George said, looking at Sunny inquiringly and a little doubtfully. At that moment, Sunny resembled less an erstwhile boxer than an emaciated shepherd.

"Well, Timmy exaggerates my accomplishments as he tends to do, but, yes, for a time in my life, I took boxing quite seriously," Sunny said. "And at one pernt, my brothers Frank, who we called Brother, and Ralph, who we called Peanuts, and I, we did form our own club and built a ring inside of a diner."

"A diner?" Plimpton said. "It must have been rather large to accommodate a boxing ring!"

"Well, what happened, George, is that they had taken out the booths. It was a beautiful diner of the old-fashioned kind with the quilted stainless steel that had been abandoned after the war. It stood on an empty lot next to our house. So, we'd charge neighborhood kids to come watch fights that had previously taken place on the streets, aye? For ring ropes we had used rope ladders like those that hung from the side of barges. The thing is, they had been dipped in pine tar which made them highly flammable, and one day Brother left a burning cigarette next to the ring and by the time the fire department arrived there was nothing left of our boxing club but charred stools and blackened chrome.

"I really was never very good at it," Sunny continued with little pause, "but boxing was an important part of the growing part of being a kid. I don't know the circumstances of your own childhood, George, but for us in Red Hook, boxing allowed us to travel to different neighborhoods, to meet people who weren't like us. When I consider that experience now, what boxing really served to do is to give me my first taste of theater."

"Theater?" George asked. I was beginning to feel like a spectator at Flushing Meadows.

"Yes. In fact, the first role that I ever got was right here at BAM. I had just returned from the hospital where I had been recovering from gangrene after shooting myself in the leg and my father drove me to an audition for a company called the

Tophatters. It was my first audition and I got the part. It was a Saroyan play, I forget the name of it, but I remember the director being a pretentious son of a bitch. He'd smoke a cigarette and if the cigarette was four inches long, the ash was three and a half. You really have to work on it to smoke a cigarette without disturbing the ashes! But I can say that the foundation of my desire to act was born of my experiences as a young fighter. You got in the ring, the ref called out your name, all the people were looking up at you, the adrenaline was rushing. The experience of the boxing ring is quite magnificent. If you do your work, you're never scared and you're never a loser in boxing. Or in theater. I turned out to be a hell of a lot better actor than I was a fighter, though. And theater was safer—you didn't get the shit knocked out of you!"

"My word!" said Plimpton, who was now regarding Sunny in a somewhat spellbound way. I had seen that look before—in a photograph of Plimpton sitting near ringside on the night Ali stopped Foreman in the eighth round in Kinshasa. "I want to hear all about that. There is a long history of boxers who went on to become actors. Victor McLaglen, the great Jake LaMotta, of course. Even my nemesis Archie Moore, who I am sorry to say just passed away, did a bit of acting. There have been quite a few, though none of them were very good at it. They turned out to have been a hell of a lot better fighters than actors."

Both men laughed and were so obviously enjoying each other's company that if I had slipped away at that moment, they would have carried on without pause. But I wouldn't have wanted to miss a word.

"Listen, I don't know what I'm doing here," George said. "You ought to be the one going onstage instead of me. I'm in charge and whatever I say goes. If you would like to get up there and talk about boxing, about Brooklyn, about Red Hook, about pretentious directors, about whatever you like, you say the word."

Sunny smiled and said thank you, but that he had come only to listen that night and it wouldn't be fair to take away the time from the people who had prepared their stories.

Plimpton bid us goodbye with a slight bow and the promise to Sunny that he would one day visit him at his bar. We stayed for two of the speakers before leaving during a break. Sunny easily became fidgety when he was required to remain still without a cigarette. Sitting through an entire movie was torment and although he liked to go to plays above all, he often tired of the experience by the intermission and was grateful at the suggestion that we leave.

On the car ride home, Sunny was still quite high. He began talking about all the prominent people he had met in his life—mostly artists but also actors and musicians—and how he had nearly always come away from these experiences deeply disappointed. Bruce Dern, whom he befriended after he returned from California, had been as low-minded and coarse in real life as he usually was on the screen. But he was merely a garden-variety lout compared to Larry Rivers. Allen Ginsberg came across as a huckster. Janis Joplin and Jimi Hendrix had left him indifferent, though he admitted that he had been only vaguely familiar with their music. He might have been genuinely charmed by Frankie Lymon, who was sitting on the lap of Nina Simone at a party he once attended, but he'd never had a chance to speak to either one. The greatest disillusionment of all had come at the hands of spiritual charlatans during his years in India.

"And as a consequence of these experiences, I tend not to be starstruck anymore," Sunny said as we pulled up to the bar. "So I'm glad for tonight because George Plimpton—he didn't disappoint me, aye? I was really taken by him, Timmy. He was sort of an exaggeration of himself. With his big hair, his suit, his accent. But what I will remember about this day is that he was so kindly. And he loved you. He stopped doing what he was doing to pay homage and respect to you and I liked that because I love you, too. Me, I would always pay homage and respect to you. But who am I? I'm just Sunny. The fact that *he* did it—this is George Plimpton. I know he's not better than I, not worse than I, but he wasn't full of himself, aye? I don't think I'll ever forget how he invited me to get up on that stage. He didn't have to extend himself in the way that he did. He was humble, he had a big heart, and he had a sweet and gentle manner about himself. That's how I will always remember him."

"Knowing George, I can say that he would be very pleased with that description of him. But, Sunny . . . you shot yourself?"

"That's another story, Timmy. Remind me to tell it to you someday. Good night, my friend. And thank you. That experience we shared tonight was one of the great pleasures of my life."

George Plimpton never did get around to visiting the bar. I would see him a few more times in the years before his death and each time, he asked about "that most extraordinary man" in the solicitous manner that was so distinctive of him. He died in his sleep on a Friday morning and a photograph of him stood next to a candle that night at Sunny's.

20

No Guru, No Method,
No Teacher

SUNNY RETURNED TO NEW YORK AT THE BEGINNING OF 1957 after being honorably discharged three months shy of his completed tour of duty. Although he was a trained aircraft engine mechanic and had been offered a job at the San Bernardino airport, a different path had begun to take shape in his mind during his final months in the service. Friends had taken him to a sneak preview of *Giant* that fall and James Dean's Jett Rink had been a revelation. Notwithstanding that he later identified his adolescent experiences in the ring as his first taste of the stage, the idea of actually becoming an actor hadn't really begun to take shape until then.

After his successful audition with the Tophatters, Brooklyn's oldest theater group, the director pressed a copy of Constantin Stanislavski's *An Actor Prepares* into his hands. Sunny began to understand that a serious study of acting was as rigorous and formal as the learning of any craft. On the advice of a fellow actor, he began taking lessons with Eli Rill, a teacher affiliated with Lee Strasberg's Actors Studio. He studied sense memory techniques. Emotional recall techniques. He did vocal exercises and made character studies. He wrote short sketches, which he performed in small productions—living rooms often serving as playhouses.

In time, he would befriend Ellen Stewart, the founder of Café La MaMa, the preeminent off-off-Broadway theater, and though he took part in various productions there and elsewhere, he would never make a career of acting unless one considers running a bar a kind of stagecraft. He would later say that acting was a passion interrupted by another passion. He didn't make much distinction between the various artistic disciplines. Theater, painting, drawing, collage-work, making music—they were all "art" and in his view, an artist might become proficient in each of these like a ballplayer who has mastered every position. A generalist. After all, he had continued working as a jeweler during this period, at the same store that had employed him as a teenager, and he now took up drawing and painting with the same zeal that he showed for drama. Acting was something that was done communally; painting was done alone, and as he began to realize he was most content in his own company, particularly when he could lose himself in work, he devoted ever more time to his canvases.

Although the 1950s and '60s were New York's most productive artistic period, he wasn't aware of the currents that had made the city the hub of the contemporary art world. He knew as little about Philip Guston as he knew about Jasper Johns, Helen Frankenthaler, color field painting, or action painting. He found his early schooling not in museums and galleries but in churches. His first themes were religious—Madonnas, saints, and crucifixions—and his depictions were figurative. He came across a copy of *Death in the Afternoon* and began making studies from the photographs of bullfighters included in the book. It would take him years, as he would tell me later, to get beyond painting what the eye sees and to understand the thought process behind abstractions. While many of his contemporaries were expanding their consciousness through psychedelic agents, something Sunny always shunned, his doors of perception would gradually be opened by the brushstrokes of Willem de Kooning.

A café owner he befriended asked him to hang his work in his shop, which led to his first commission. In exchange for free meals of lamb provençal and coq au vin, he spent a year creating landscape murals for a newly opened restaurant on the Upper East Side called Le Boeuf a la Mode, the kind of place where the clientele might have stepped out of a Louis Auchincloss novel. The owner, Etienne, encouraged him to paint in the evenings while the well-heeled patrons were dining, so as to be a novel attraction in his own right: "the artist at work." He soon began receiving private commissions for portraiture by some of the regular customers, one of whom, a department store heiress named Alice, would become his patron and intermittent lover for over a decade, though she was more than twice his age.

He was living in an apartment near Brooklyn College then and occasionally socialized with students he met at a neighborhood art supply store. Evenings when he wasn't at work in Manhattan, he often had jazz musicians come over to play in his living room and one such night, he was introduced to a psychology student named Frederica—Fredi, for short. The two became romantically involved very quickly and decided to marry in short order. It was 1963. She was black and the notion of being involved with a woman of a different race was entirely taboo in his old neighborhood. But when he told his father of his plans, Ralph only asked, "Do you love her?"

Sunny and Fredi moved to Bleecker Street in the West Village and soon had a daughter they named Tracy. In the afternoons, Sunny would take the two in his camper bus to the Rockaways in Queens, a revolver tucked into his beach bag in case anyone gave the mixed-race family any trouble. Fredi was grounded and earnest, her mind on family and earning a Ph.D. at New York University, while Sunny was decidedly undomestic in his routines, becoming increasingly caught up in socializing with other artists and drinking heavily. His customary outfit in those years was an Abercrombie & Fitch safari suit, of which he owned several, and at night, wearing this Hemingwayesque getup, he went to Fanelli's in SoHo, the Cedar Street Tavern, and, particularly, Max's Kansas City. Every generation of New York artists, except our own, seems to have its celebrated watering holes, but at the time, Sunny merely thought of them as places where one could drink and hang out with like-minded people. He began dividing his time between Bleecker Street and a loft on Wooster Street, paid for by Alice, his uptown benefactress. His marriage soon deteriorated. He would later say that he had an unmatrimonial constitution. By Sunny's accounts, this seemed to be a common condition at the time. One night at Max's, he met a Greek woman named Catherine, an heiress as well and herself recently divorced. She had married a Venizélos, the most famous political family in Greece—the closest American equivalent would be a Kennedy—but by the time she met Sunny, she was an acolyte of an unknown Indian guru named Acharya Rajneesh.

Catherine went home with Sunny the first night they met, joining a carousel of mistresses that made his romantic life a complicated juggling act. While maintaining relationships with Fredi and Alice, he had also impregnated a sometime girlfriend named Mary, who only stayed long enough for Sunny to name the newborn Paul, after Cézanne, before moving back to California. Paul and Sunny wouldn't see each other for another thirty years, a span of time their relationship never could entirely overcome.

There were countless other passing entanglements. It wasn't unusual for Sunny to be with three women in a single day. In the mornings he would try to remember the lies he told the night before. He thought to himself more than once, "Everyone thinks I'm in love with them and meantime, I don't have a clear enough heart to love anything. I'm just satisfying my desires, a prisoner to the stories I'm telling." After he was given a book on St. Francis, he briefly considered becoming a Franciscan monk. He also dabbled in Krishnamurti and Meister Eckhart—this was the 1960s, after all. When Catherine said that she would like to make a gift to him by buying him a plane ticket to India to meet her spiritual teacher, Sunny was ready to go.

He arrived in Bombay in the company of two nuns who had left their convent. Like Sunny, they were on a spiritual journey. He had little money; his luggage contained his safari suits, several dozen boxes of Wheatena cereal, a number of carefully wrapped jars of honey, and a supply of razor blades to last several years. Sunny was tremendously fond of Wheat-

ena which, along with honey and razor blades, he had been
told would be hard to find in India. The customs agents gath-
ered around his open suitcases in suspicious bewilderment,
chattering amongst themselves, until Sunny presented each
with a box and assured them it would help with their diges-
tions. They were exceedingly appreciative and, with several
bows, he was allowed into India.

Although eager to see this land that was mysterious and
full of fantasies that he had created for himself, he had developed a tremendous cold on the airplane and he took a taxi to
an apartment that Catherine rented in the Breach Candy section of the city and promptly went to sleep for three days. He
woke to a clanging sound and looked out the open window to
see a boy with bandy legs bicycling away, milk cans banging
against his wheels. He went outside and began walking and it
seemed as though in three days' sleep he had been transported
back three centuries. Servants slept on mats in stairwells and
street vendors served food in cones of newspaper or leaf. Tur-
baned dentists sat on the ground in lotus position with their
implements laid out on blankets in front of them. There were
ox-carts in the streets and the cars appeared to run not on
gasoline but on horns. Although the city was very poor, there
was little garbage—everything seemed to be consumed.
There was a great abundance of rats but in this upside-down
world he had entered, they were revered, not hunted. To his
amazement, they perched carefree on walls in broad daylight
and scuttered untroubled amongst the legs of people sitting at
outdoor restaurants.

He remained in Bombay for several weeks before taking
a train to Rajasthan, a mountainous state in the northwestern
part of the country, where Rajneesh had set up a meditation

camp in a place called Mount Abu. He had yet to call himself Bhagwan Rajneesh, the name by which much of the world would come to know him. At sunrise on the morning after his arrival, Sunny rose to join the other disciples in their daily meditation exercises, imagining that he would be sitting cross-legged, contemplating otherworldly matters. Instead, he soon found himself hopping on the balls of his feet while making owl-like cries (*hoo hoo hoo*). He also, at various times, panted with rapid shallow breaths, thrashed about epileptically, and lay on the ground in a state of outright exhaustion. All the while, a balding, heavily bearded man addressed the group, from his perch on an armchair, with a lilting Indian accent. "Act upon any impulse you have," he said, as some pounded the floor with their fists. Others writhed and jiggled. Many howled. "This is catharsis," he continued. "If you want to scream, scream. If you want to cry or laugh or beat the earth, cry or laugh or beat the earth. If you want to tear your clothes off, tear them off. If you want to copulate in the dust, copulate in the dust. Once an impulse has been expressed, one is free of it. Madness is the lack of expression of insanity. In order to become sane one first has to become mad."

Though he never would copulate in the dust, Sunny took to his meditation with great diligence, often performing the hour-long exercise both morning and night. And Rajneesh took to Sunny, recognizing in him a highly charismatic personality with a gift for language, someone who could be an effective proselytizer. He gave him a new name, Swami Dharmananda, as the mark of being a sannyasin—an initiate. Soon "Swami Dharmananda" was invited to private audiences and to sit alongside Rajneesh onstage, to travel by train to the homes of wealthy benefactors, and to be seen as his right-hand man. Sunny had never met anyone so learned. Rajneesh's apartment back in Bombay included a vast library containing thousands of books—so many books that one needed to climb a rolling ladder to reach many of them—and Rajneesh claimed to have read them all. He would call himself the most educated person in the world. His lectures, given while sitting perfectly still in an armchair, touched on all manner of philosophy, psychology, history, and literature. He was equally likely to reference Freud, the Upanishads, or Tolstoy. Sunny was unfamiliar with Russian literature, theories of psychoanalysis, the precepts of Jainism, and many of the arcane subjects on which the discourses touched, but he became convinced that he was in the presence of an extraordinary mind—or at least one that possessed a photographic memory.

Sunny did not spend all of his time in Mount Abu. He

traveled in the countryside and Alice regularly wired him money, with which he rented an apartment in Bombay and returned to New York periodically, though seeing little of his daughter, Tracy, and his estranged wife. (Fredi never would forgive him for his straying ways early in their marriage.) Wearing his orange pajamas and beaded necklace while walking about in Greenwich Village, he was often mistaken for a Hare Krishna. In Washington Square Park, he played the bongo drums. He also proselytized and persuaded and opened the eyes of future sannyasins. He never went home to Red Hook on these visits either, feeling entirely estranged from that world. How could he explain to his childhood friends that he had become the consigliere to a man who wore tunics, denounced social conditioning, and championed sexual liberation?

In India, the scales fell from Sunny's eyes little by little. As the number of followers of Rajneesh grew from a few dozen into the hundreds, he began to recognize the same sorts of jealousies, the same envies, among the other sannyasins that he had encountered in the New York art world. A spiritual competitiveness as to who was the most enlightened. And Rajneesh, too, began to disenchant him.

He had already overheard him advising wealthy Western women to marry Indian acolytes from his inner circle, ceding their names and their bank accounts. He couldn't help but notice that for a spiritual guide, Rajneesh seemed to have an uncommon regard for treasure. He wore a diamond-covered watch and though he only drove a humble Impala, he often mentioned a desire to upgrade. He would, in time, acquire a Mercedes and a fleet of Rolls-Royces numbering more than ninety. When one of his disciples' teenage daughters asked

Rajneesh whether he thought it was a good idea for her to smuggle hashish out of the country, Rajneesh replied, "If you have the impulse to do it, do it. That which is within your system must be expressed, but be willing to suffer the consequences—along with the consequences you will find a truth that will bring you to a higher consciousness." Privately, Sunny began to have serious doubts as to the quality of advice the sannyasins were receiving.

On a trip back to New York, Sunny learned of the discovery of endorphins and a phenomenon called the runner's high, and he recalled how at the end of the dynamic meditation exercises, when the sannyasins had collapsed to the ground from exhaustion, Rajneesh would say, "Now you feel the state of grace descending upon you." Was it grace, he now wondered, or more earthly hormones that were descending on them? In fact, the thought had crossed his mind more than once that Rajneesh often seemed less holy than wholly out of it, as if he had been smoking opium. In the early days, Sunny had always sat in the front row at Rajneesh's lectures, eager to show his devotion, but as his doubts grew and he began to feel that he had been used, he found himself moving farther and farther toward the back of the lecture hall.

By the time the day came when Rajneesh gave a talk on modern art, Sunny was sitting in the last row. He was practically sitting outside. Sunny hadn't always understood all the recondite topics that Rajneesh touched on during his discourses, but he knew something about the history of modern art. And when Rajneesh began equating the distortion of images in Georges Braque and Pablo Picasso's paintings with the loss of values in the West, Sunny said in his mind, "This guy has no idea. He has no idea as to the concepts that went into the creation of these images." Sunny had been enthralled by Picasso and the evolution of his theories from the early blue period to his African period and Cubism and the surrealism of his later years, and to hear Rajneesh talk so ignorantly about the matter dashed whatever remained of the admiration he had once felt for him. He went back to his room and composed a letter denouncing Rajneesh as a spiritual Pied Piper and a fraud. He mailed his denunciation to a Bombay newspaper; soon after it was published, the two former nuns with whom he had first traveled to India came to warn him that there was a plot on his life. By then, Rajneesh traveled with a cadre of sullen bodyguards armed with pistols and Sunny did not need further persuading. He packed his few belongings and left his room that same night, and soon was on a plane destined for New York, turning his back on Rajneesh and all organized religion.

Sunny tried to resume his former way of life, returning to Max's Kansas City, now in its second incarnation. Alice, his friend and patron, who had supported him all these years, died not long after he returned and left him a rich sum of money, which he kept stowed in a dresser drawer and would spend in a year's time on drinking and passing friendships. He felt intensely lonely and adrift. India had ended on a bad note for him, and he now viewed the time he spent there as a failed attempt at taking a shortcut to spiritual contentment. (The only sense of contentment he had ever really felt was in the act of making art. He thought of it as making friendship with art—what effort one put into one's work, the work gave back.)

In 1978, he returned to Red Hook and with his remaining $3000 bought a tiny house not far from the bar above which his father and mother still lived. He had never expected to return to the neighborhood, but the familiarity of his parents and his childhood home provided some semblance of substance to his life. His uncle still opened the bar at dawn to serve breakfast and Sunny settled into a routine of coming in around noon and helping with the lunchtime and afternoon customers, who were nearly all steadies, while his father sat in the back room taking numbers for bookies. An intensely honest man, Ralph, now in his seventies, would play regulars' numbers (it was customary to have a lucky number) even when they didn't personally come in to place bets, and pay out the winnings if the number hit.

It was a quiet and uninterrupted existence that Sunny would maintain through his father's death in 1987 and right up till Uncle John died seven years later, not long before we met.

Rajneesh, meanwhile, fled tax collectors, first turning up in New Jersey (all crooks seem to head for Jersey at some point, except those already living in Jersey), and eventually the Pacific Northwest. He died in 1990. Once or twice, in more recent years, Sunny had come face-to-face with customers who were wearing the telltale beaded malas of Rajneesh's true believers, but he didn't let on. Sunny had always considered paranoia to be merely a form of prudence. As far as he knew, the hit Rajneesh placed on him was never lifted.

21

Good Friday

As WITH ANYONE OPERATING OUTSIDE THE LAW FOR A long time, we were very conscious of the ephemerality of our situation. It was like conducting a secret love affair that is destined to be found out, but one cannot bring oneself to break it off until it has run its course. In the spring of 2001, Red Hook still felt as uncharted as the night I had first stepped into the bar. Wild dogs with lycanthropic tendencies even now terrorized bicyclists reckless enough to traverse the most shadowed stretches of the neighborhood at night, and in the mornings one still came across charred wrecks left like oblations to whatever saint watches over car thieves. When one other solitary bar opened on a lonesome corner a quarter mile away, Sunny was outwardly supportive but privately uneasy, anxious that the existence of an actual licensed bar would bring unwanted attention by city officials on the neighborhood.

The authorities were not unacquainted with Sunny's.

When the Bureau of Alcohol, Tobacco, and Firearms agents who had moved into an unmarked fortified building nearby several years earlier came to drink their beers, they did so inconspicuously and unobtrusively, happy to be collaborationists. Two plainclothes officers in an unmarked police car had driven slowly by the bar on many Friday nights, stopping to say hello if Sunny or I happened to be standing outside. They were sociable in the way a beat cop from an earlier era might be. "How's the night going?" "You're not having any trouble with anybody?" "Starks or Sprewell?" (If they had only asked "Klimt or Klee?" they would have gotten an impassioned disquisition on the subject.)

The end came abruptly, in the form of a police van that pulled up to the bar on the evening of Good Friday. Sunny signaled for the band to keep playing so the customers wouldn't grow uneasy and he went outside to greet the officers. But these officers were strangers and they asked different kinds of questions. They were unhappy when Sunny handed them an outdated floor plan. They disapproved of the expired occupancy permit. They frowned at the dancing they observed through the window. They blanched when Sunny failed to produce a valid liquor license. They ordered the bar shut on the spot.

Shaken, but not overly so—Sunny embodied his name about as well as anyone this side of Busty Heart and Boston Shorty—he cheerily announced that this was merely an opportunity to get the paperwork in order and reopen under his own name. Not John's Bar, as the expired documents had had it, but Sunny's.

The following Friday we sat by the front door in the dark, turning customers away. Another van pulled up, this time delivering ATF agents who presented Sunny with a warrant and combed the bar and basement, presumably for signs of speakeasy activity. While it wasn't exactly Eliot Ness and a team of axe-wielding Prohibition agents destroying barrels of moonshine (indeed, the men seemed slightly ashamed), this follow-up raid left Sunny uncharacteristically spooked.

He began to mistrust phone lines and whenever he wanted to discuss bar business or anything else that he regarded as private, he would ask that I come see him in person. He no longer considered the bar safe for such discussions either, and when I'd arrive he would say, "Let's go sit," and lead me outside to the old Pontiac that he had inherited from his uncle. Although Sunny might not have been in the mob, he seemed to have studied their customs carefully. He liked to get in back, roll the windows down, stretch one leg out on the seat, and smoke while I sat up front behind the wheel. I never actually put the key in the ignition and if a professional eavesdropper had been listening in they might have been intrigued, but not for professional reasons. They would have overheard accounts of thievery (liberating a safe from a nearby shipping company office with a forklift, a crime that remains unsolved a half-century later), travel (riding alone on beautifully painted steam locomotives through the Indian countryside with no real destination), and exotic amatory rituals (biting into an apple each time climax arrived, at the insistence of a Japanese lover). They also would have heard an appreciation of Piero Manzoni, the late Milanese artist best known for his works *Artist's Breath* (balloons containing his exhalations) and *Artist's Shit* (tin cans whose contents have never been verified), and a lamentation for the premature death of Tiger

Flowers, the Bible-clutching middleweight champion from Georgia whose very name deserves resurrection.

For all his secretiveness, Sunny really just wanted to shoot the breeze in his typically scattershot fashion and I was more than happy to indulge him. But one day he abruptly confided that he had another reason to get out of the house for a bit. "Tone has been needing some space, Timmy. You see, she's been experiencing morning sickness."

I turned to look at him over my shoulder and he was grinning sheepishly.

"Yes, it surprised me as much as it probably surprises you to learn that everything down there still works. I was ready to . . . you know, contain myself, and she said, 'No, Sunny. This one is for me.' I never expected this to happen to me again but I'm going to be a papa."

It would be the quietest summer and, for a week and a half, the quietest September in years. I continued to take the train each morning to my job in Manhattan, where I had risen, less by initiative than by the occasional updrafts that jettison higher-ups while sucking up those below, from clerical foot soldier to editor and sometime writer. My office had moved across town into the city's newest skyscraper, a granite and glass tower at the foot of Times Square hailed variously as avant-garde, state-of-the-art, and forward-thinking. At its base, a video screen curled along an eleven-story turret relaying the minute-to-minute fortunes of the financial markets as well as round-the-clock communications from the advertising world to passersby below. A sharp-eyed visitor, aided by binoculars, might have caught sight of me seated in my office just beyond the screen's upper right-hand corner—desk, chair, light, and air all ergonomic, of course. A *Blade Runner* future had arrived in small measure and I seemed to be in it.

Indoors, we breathed an atmosphere cleaner, we were told, than Iceland's. Though the rumor that the washroom urinals were handmade in Sesto Fiorentino turned out to be unfounded, another—that it would have taken the entire citizenry of Tuvalu three years to pay for our gaudy lunchroom—turned out to be true. It was a spectacle of undulating blue titanium ceilings and billowing Italian blown-glass walls designed by the preeminent maestro of undulating and billowing architecture.

Sunny's had served as my private counterweight to this rarified realm (there is only so much sophistication that one can put up with in the course of a week) and to compensate for its sudden absence in my life, I rented a second apartment in Red Hook to which I would regularly retreat several evenings a week and on the weekends. It was not lost on me that while others rented summer bungalows in the Hamptons or the Catskills, I found my haven next door to a bus garage in Red Hook. I was seeking escape of a different sort. I furnished the single large room with one table and two chairs from the bar, and three of Sunny's paintings. My imagination supplied the sounds and faces.

On the morning of the eleventh, I watched the distant collapsing diorama and heard the confused cries of responders on a police scanner from a Brooklyn rooftop. All that day, ashes and scraps of paper drifted across the river like churned-up flakes in a snow globe. By night, the view of the city from Brooklyn's Promenade was dreamlike—smoky and strangely

silent. A Kurosawa set piece. The only sign of life in the harbor came from the swirling sapphire lights of anchored police
boats ringing the Battery in a half-moon formation. Sunny's
first reaction had been to run to his basement to retrieve an
ancient gun he had hidden there, prepared to protect his
home and family, though from what he wasn't sure. But when
I called him that evening, he sounded reflective, as if he had
already internalized the events.

"These things that we're seeing and experiencing," he
said, "they're not new to me, Timmy. They bring to mind
other moments in my life. These ashes that came down from
the sky, they reminded me of my childhood. They reminded
me of Election Days.

"As children we didn't know politics but we knew about
fires. In the weeks leading up to Election Day we would scav-
enge the whole neighborhood for planks, pallets, any kind of
wood we could get our hands on. People would stand outside
their houses and guard their wooden fences because everything that was wood would be taken. All of Red Hook did
this, which to me meant that all of New York did this. After
dark on Election Day, on all the street corners leading into
the neighborhood, little fires were lit as diversions to keep the
fire department from reaching the main fire, which would be
built right on the next street corner outside the bar. The
grown-ups would throw ropes over lampposts and swing ef-
figies of the politicians we weren't supposed to like—Dewey,
O'Dwyer—over the flames until they lit. It was very dramatic. Walking to school the mornings after Election Day,
the entire neighborhood would smell like burnt wood and
saturated ashes. These were joyous occasions and what has
taken place today is terrible, but there was something in the

experience of looking up and seeing these ashes floating down today that made me think life is repeating itself."

Sunny had never been a reader and he didn't have much use for newscasts or televised experts to account for days such as this. He would sooner take one image, a bit or fragment, and compare it to past moments in his life in order to make sense of an experience. Maybe this is what is meant when someone is said to have a painterly eye. That night, Sunny's seemed as reasonable as any other interpretation of the day's events.

In November, I drove Sunny to the hospital to pick up Tone, whom he had married on the quiet earlier that year, and their new daughter, Oda Sophia. I would see little of them that winter. It was a subdued time in the city. I made halfhearted visits to other spots—the Lion's Head in the Village and Marion's on the Bowery, the Woods Inn in Glendale and Lento's in Bay Ridge, but they left little lasting impression and I soon gave up on trying to reproduce a Friday night at Sunny's. It wasn't bars, not even venerable ones, that I was missing.

Sunny's quietly reopened in April, licensed and otherwise licit, and most of the old customers streamed back with the relief of squirrels who had been evicted from Central Park while the trees had been closed for renovations. I had not been the only one who had had no other place to go. Reclaiming their favorite spots, they appraised the changes the bar had undergone in a year and for a time, the wisdom of each refurbishment was a frequent topic of discussion. Few took exception to the freshly painted walls or mourned the decades of dust that had been wiped off the ceiling fans, and only one or two submitted that the sealing of the rat holes in the basement was a bad idea as it would force the wayward critters up into the bar in search for a new egress. A Czech photographer named George, who had made historic New York bars the central subject of his work and had probably visited more of them than any native son, complained that the mechanical whir of the new ice machine beneath the bar added a white noise to the room that was disruptive to the bar's "exquisite melancholy"—a grievance I privately agreed with.

"It sounds like bastard offspring of Zamboni!" he said.

Whereas in the "old Sunny's" one mostly had only to decide between liquors, not brands, when ordering a drink, the back bar of the "new Sunny's" was now lined with a modest selection of different whiskeys, gins, vodkas, and rums. Gazing at the array of labels one night, Paul, the onetime bakery-truck driver from Maine and balladeer of the Jericho Turnpike, said, "Staas are staas to me. I don't need to know their names. Same with whiskey. When I come to Sunny's, I don't want to have to say 'Give me this or give me that.' 'A shot' has always been good enough and should always be good enough." A holdover from the days of Uncle John, Paul was the single most quarrelsome man I had ever met. He never would come to accept that time's progress had arrived at Sunny's and, by and by, he came less and less.

After James Cagney went missing (presumably not by his own locomotion), the statuettes of the Marx Brothers and Bogart and their fellow Hollywood luminaries were collected and lined up side by side on a shelf above the bar, as if forever giving a final curtain call. Opposite, on the wall over the booths, hung three large new canvases—paintings that Sunny had been working on over the winter and had decided to leave on display. Although they were abstract in style, some were soon playing a parlor game called Find the Hidden Penises in Sunny's Paintings. There were more than a few.

Not all the changes at Sunny's were skin-deep. Some were profound. Drinks were now priced as they would be at any bar and the honor-system chits were put away into a drawer beneath the cash register like commemorations of another era. Coming to realize that conducting a legal business had hidden costs, Sunny and Tone decided to open up on Saturdays as well. And after meeting a young Cooper Union graduate and amateur electrician named Francis who appeared in need of some direction in life, they asked whether he would like to run the bar on Wednesday nights. Francis admitted he had no bartending experience and Sunny said that was to his credit. An actual bartender from County Galway had once briefly worked at Sunny's until he took it upon himself to put the beer on ice one night and Sunny said it would be better if he returned to the customer side of the bar. If anything got a rise out of Sunny, it was this sort of innovative thinking.

To the traditionalists, with whom I was a fellow traveler, these developments were heresy. Sunny had always maintained that it was his firm belief that the less something was available, the more desirable it became—a convincing theory usually applied to sex but one that Sunny had appropriated brilliantly for his bar as well. Opening a couple more nights might seem innocent enough, a reasonable proposition in the conventional business world, but threatened to make the experience of going to Sunny's just a little less rarified, a little more commonplace. "Going to Sunny's used to be an event that one looked forward to all week," grumbled my friend

Chris, who had met his wife at the bar. After a few more drinks he declared, "Sunny's is dead," though he would continue to return for years to come, apparently preferring to spend his time in a necropolis than in bars that aroused in him no passions at all.

A more reasoned judgment came from the eldest regular customer of Sunny's, a staunch leftist named Charlie King who usually arrived very late, hoping to encounter either a shapely divorcee or a Republican to divert his attention from his chronic insomnia. He had recently begun walking with a cane after some kids in the neighborhood sicced their pit bulls on him for the spectacle. Overhearing the new Sunny's versus the old Sunny's debate one night, Charlie, with Guinness froth on his Airedale mustache, weighed in by saying, "A woman in a picket line in Baltimore once expressed something so philosophically brilliant to me. She said, 'Eat shit if you must, but never call it ice cream.' You don't do a brainwashing of yourself. Confronted with conflict, you compromise but you don't deceive yourself that you're doing something else. You make compromises but you don't sell out. And as far as I'm concerned, Sunny might have made a few changes but he hasn't sold out."

After a reflective pause, he smirked and said, "By the way, the tragedy of my own life is not that I sold out, but that no one ever made me an offer."

22

The Great Criminal
Hugh Hefner

My Sweet Tooth Says I Wanna,
My Wisdom Tooth Says No.
—FLETCHER HENDERSON

ONE NIGHT THE DOOR OPENED AND A WOMAN ENtered with such theatricality that everyone turned to look her way. She was the kind of woman often described as maddeningly beautiful. As most men with a certain amount of life experience can attest, spend enough time with a woman who possesses this quality and eventually the balance is tipped—either the spell she casts dissipates and one finds her merely gorgeous but no longer unnervingly so, or the pendulum swings in the other direction and she causes one to lose one's equilibrium altogether.

Trailed by a retinue of a half-dozen men and parting the crowd with her looks, she walked directly to where I stood behind the bar and leaned over until her lips were a finger's width from my face. "I want you to make me a drink," she said. "And then I want you to dance with me."

Chester Burnett stopped singing, the world stopped turning for a tick, and when it resumed, Jimmy Dorsey's "Amapola" came on, the kind of song that always ought to be playing when a great beauty has commanded you to dance with her. It was October but she was wearing a July dress. I came around the side of the bar and she put her hands around my neck and pulled herself into me with the reserve of Mata Hari. Although the burble of conversation had resumed, it was lost on no one that the bartender and a femme fatale who had appeared as in a dream were now slowly revolving like a music box couple in the middle of the barroom. I kept my eyes cast down lest they catch anyone's gaze but through the chatter I recognized the voice of Buzz, a working-class laborer on the trading floor of the New York Stock Exchange, named either for his basic-training haircut or his cutting commentary.

"Someone's thinking of baseball."

"Probably counting presidents, too," added his constant sidekick, Tom.

She clung to me like I was holding the only umbrella in town during a monsoon. I attempted to make conversation to break the tension.

"Who are you?" I said.

She buried her face in my neck.

"Where did you come from?"

Her clutch tightened. I was sure I smelled poppy flowers. Talking to her was like talking to the moon. Silence was my only answer.

The words "I'm Tim" had never sounded more feeble than they did at that moment.

If she had held me closer, she would have been behind me.

"Nora," she whispered when the song came to its end. "From New Orleans." She turned and disappeared into the crowd.

Sunny clucked when I stepped back behind the bar. "My goodness, what a candy store life can be," he said.

"I had an idea once for the opening sentence of a book that I never wrote," I said. " 'She was my Mount Vesuvius, I was her Pompeii.' Sunny . . . you're looking at Pompeii."

"May I say, Timmy, you do look a little ashen at the moment."

I went back to opening beers and pouring drinks and washing glasses, and a little later Nora reappeared with her men in tow and, without a parting glance, left as abruptly as she had arrived, a tropical depression churning back toward the Gulf.

These kinds of things more often happened to Sunny, not me. Once I overheard a woman ask whether Sunny would look at her new butterfly tattoo and he agreed, not realizing until she unzipped her pants that the butterfly was located about six inches below her navel. He dutifully examined the tattoo and had the composure to say that it was an exceedingly good rendition of a butterfly and that it reminded him of a lesser-known Warhol.

Another night, a brunette born some years after Watergate followed him into the back room, where he had gone to sit alone and smoke during the early evening quiet, and announced, "I've been in New York for five days and when I saw you through the window before coming in, I said to myself, 'That's the first good-looking man I've seen since I left Texas.' I think we should make love right now."

Without giving Sunny time to formulate a diplomatic reply, she pushed him backward and in one continuous motion, straddled his lap, unclasped her bra, and pulled his hand beneath her shirt. Although Sunny was far from the most self-possessed man I had ever known, he had often shown the ability to think on the fly and to exhibit grace under pressure even in cases where the pressure was being brought to bear brazenly on his lap.

"It would be good, certainly," he said, "but . . . it wouldn't look good, aye?" The woman slowly nodded in a resigned way and, with a sigh, slid off him, adjusting her clothes.

After she had left in search of other pleasures and Sunny was sure the coast was clear, he came back to the bar where a small chorus of throat clearing erupted. I had been serving Joe, the bar philanthropist, and a row of his cronies up from Bay Ridge. Sunny smiled apologetically, as if he was returning to a dugout after whiffing at the plate with three runners aboard.

"That was nutsy," he said, pouring himself a shot. "This beautiful woman desiring me. How is a man not supposed to respond to that?"

"Uh, Sunny . . . most men do," said Joe, arching his eyebrows and giving Sunny a meaningful look over the rim of his glasses.

"You're probably right, Joey. I told her that as much as I

would like to do what it is that it is that she wanted us to do, it wouldn't make a very good impression on the customers. But I have to confess I only said it that way so as not to hurt her feelings. The truth of the matter is, at that moment I could only think of my wife sleeping next door, my baby girl sleeping next door, and I couldn't respond in the way that she wanted me to respond. I couldn't do it. Without elaborating, you get the gist of what I'm saying. We don't want to put ourselves in situations we're going to regret tomorrow."

The men bowed their heads, a little sheepish at their lowmindedness.

"But, Sunny. She *was* exceptional!" one of Joe's friends said after a moment.

"Oh, fuhgeddaboudit. She was! She may have been the loveliest woman that I have ever had to rebuff. But to be the recipient of affections and not gorge on them is somehow giving up hell for heaven. It may leave you in a state of what might be called mundaneness but you don't have to carry your yesterdays, aye?"

The group murmured their agreement and a few looked at their ring fingers thoughtfully. The greater number of men (and the occasional woman) become moral relativists after their second drink.

"You might say the circumstance that I found myself in tonight was unique," Sunny said, taking a long pause and looking one by one into each of our faces again, "but I was a eunuch!" Sunny dissolved in laughter and we all joined in. He was one of those people who never laugh alone.

———

I ONCE HEARD a story about John Milton that went something like this: Milton was attending school as a teenager in the 1600s and one morning in his theology class, the schoolmaster asked each student to write an essay on the miracle at Cana, where Christ turned water into wine. The students spent the entire class scribbling with their quills—all but Milton. He looked out the window, lost in a daydream, his scroll blank in front of him. At the very end of the class, when the students had to turn in their essays, he picked up his quill and wrote: "The conscious water saw its God and blushed."

The story always stayed with me because it so well exemplified the ability to say something all at once poetic, concise, and memorable.

It was unique but I was a eunuch.

SUNNY WENT AROUND the bar and returned with the bottle of Jameson and refilled everyone's glass.

"You think he ever let the thought of Jackie stop him?" Joe said, gesturing at the bust of President Kennedy above the bar.

"Nye, not him. He was one of those. *Pensa col cazzo . . .* No self-control." He relit his cigarette. "The older you get you understand that the joy one takes in a person's sexual allure is the rarest kind. It's a pleasure that replenishes itself without end—unless you become greedy about it, aye? One never really tires of the human form. That reminds me—did I ever tell you guys about the first real nudes I saw in my life?"

In something close to unison, we all shook our heads. Sunny knew he had his audience captive.

"I was just a child." He pushed his hair back from his face and blew a puff of smoke toward the ceiling. "My brother Frank brought it to my attention that there was this particular roller coaster in Coney Island that overlooked one of the bathing houses that was for women only, and he had heard that the women would be laying out, taking in the sun with no clothes on.

"The bathing house was fenced in and you couldn't just go on the roller coaster and look down and see inside during the whole ride. Apparently there was one particular pernt, the precipice of one of the big drops, and it happened to be that this drop was closest to where the bathhouse was. So Frank came to me and said he spoke with some of the older guys and they were going to go to Coney Island and were going to keep going on this particular roller coaster to look at the women's boxes.

"We were just kids without any sexual experiences, and you know how children have an inquisitiveness about everything they're not exposed to. Well, I did go on that roller coaster with my brother and some of the other boys, and it was such a short moment that thank goodness for the imagination because you're going over the top of this hill before the big drop, you're looking down and you see this bush—but it's like a thousand miles away! You'd shout, 'There's one!' Maybe it wasn't really there, but the imagination is such—'I saw it! I saw it!' How one could be so fascinated by this little shadow between someone's legs? But we were kids and these were taboos and sex was a mystery to us. These women weren't being sexual from their pernt of view and they could have had black rags in their laps for all that we could see, but as a kid sees it, he's seeing . . . pussy." Sunny's eyes sparkled.

"Those were the first naked women I saw in my life and it might have been for only one brief moment but it's a moment that lasts a lifetime."

We sat in silence for a minute, each a little lost in his private reverie.

"Thank God for Bettie Page," Joe said finally. "And *Playboy*. Hugh Hefner must have cleared some things up for you, Sunny."

"He ruined it, Joey!" Sunny cried, slapping his palm on the bar. He was suddenly very angry. "Hugh Hefner, they should hang his ass! Sexuality was something that took place behind closed doors, something you did in your own space. That is no longer the case today and in my mind, it all started with Hugh Hefner. He planted the seed of a virus that's as bad as smallpox. Freedom with discipline is a grand thing but freedom without discipline is terrible, aye?"

He searched our faces for signs of solidarity. I thought of the hours he'd spent watching the Playboy Channel but bit my tongue.

"There's so much sweetness that is attached to the innocent who imagines," he went on. "Only those who are innocent can imagine in the way that innocents imagine. Too much knowledge doesn't leave any room to fill in the gaps. In my mind, Hugh Hefner is one of the worst criminals that has ever lived because what he did was take some of the joy out of childhood."

"Sunny, you make sex sound like paradise lost, not paradise gained."

"In a way it is, Timmy."

Sunny clinked his shot glass against each of ours. "Here's to being able and to the ability to resist! *Salut.*" And we drank.

23

The Heart of the Matter

WHATEVER CREATURE CARRIES THE COMMON MID-life crisis bit me at an exceptionally early age. I had barely reached my mid-thirties when I suddenly determined that I needed a vintage car—settling upon a 1962 Ford Fairlane whose truculent disposition would only reveal itself after I became its master. In short succession, I also fell in and out of love in the course of hours and minutes with a series of unavailable women, notwithstanding that I was already very much and very happily involved, and found myself frequently at my office window daydreaming of working out-of-doors. The usual symptoms.

I had never given more than my divided attention to my full-time job, a self-limiting approach in most lines of work. That I had ever held another job would have come as a surprise to the customers at Sunny's. I had always been slow to admit to a daytime profession, preferring to exist in people's

minds between eight P.M. and four A.M. Friday night and nowhere else. I was not alone in being unforthcoming about my
weekday whereabouts; by tacit agreement people tended to
leave their occupations at the door. It was years before I knew
this one was a labor lawyer, that one a seminarian. As one
regular said to me, "Picturing half these people in pressed
khakis and pantsuits seated behind computer monitors is like
picturing your dream girl using the facilities. You prefer to
suspend your disbelief." By Tuesdays, my thoughts would
turn to Friday, as central a day to my week as Sundays are to
a defensive lineman. Mild-mannered by temperament, as the
afternoon wore on on Fridays and anxious at the prospect of
being held up in the office late, I would transform into a
prickly clock-watcher. Others only had the 6:22 to Valhalla
to worry about; I had New York City's greatest bar to open,
to say nothing of an appointment first with my regular table
at Ferdinando's.

One such Friday, it was tersely suggested that my moon-
lighting was interfering with my work. I sputtered and huffed
as much as I was capable of huffing, which wasn't much, and
I was still mulling over this rebuke that evening while eating
my customary pasta con sarde below the gazes of Saints
Francis (Assisi) and Michael (Piazza) when Frank came over
and asked, "Wha's new?"—his usual opening gambit. It's
been said that talking over one's grievances with someone
who has a bit of distance is, on occasion, therapeutic (there is
a small fleet of cabdrivers to this day carrying news of my
personal affairs) and I proceeded to tell him about the two-
bit office squabble I'd had that day. Frank had always shown
a very genuine curiosity and fatherly concern about my life.

When I finished, he looked at me, shaking his head. "They gotta it right and they gotta it all wrong, Teem," he said in the same tone he might use if he found it necessary to point out to me that John Paul II was a member of the Roman Catholic Church. "You moonlight but not atta de bar. You moonlight atta de day job, *capisce*? Your heart, it's not in it."

I am convinced that I have benefited more from such exchanges in my adult life than I ever would have were I paying for them by the hour. By the time he brought me the limoncello he fermented in the basement for his choice regulars (bootlegging was a solitary diversion that endured in certain Red Hook circles), I had decided that the only principled thing to do was to give notice. I would be a one-day-a-week bartender at the only bar that I would ever want to work at and in due course figure out what to do with the rest of my time. And so I quit.

After spending most of the summer along the boardwalk between Brighton Beach and Seagate (another luxury I had often daydreamed about), I took up seasonal work with a rooftop gardener I knew from the bar. She turned out to be as versed in Greene as she was in greenery (she was partial to *The End of the Affair* while I had a soft spot for *Our Man in Havana*) and we liked to fill the hours by discussing whatever book we happened to be reading. Odds-on, we were the only landscapers in the city involved in an ongoing dispute over whether Lawrence or Gerald was the most talented of the Durrell brothers. Many of her clients were well-off, scions and titans who lived in the legendary apartment buildings east and west of Central Park. Forest green awnings reached from door to curb, Gaddafian doormen adding a sense of ceremony to our arrivals and departures. Service elevators took us skyward to the aeries I once imagined living in, but I had come to believe there is a certain pleasure in only briefly visiting such places to prune the deadwood before returning to earth—the wealth, in itself, being vertiginous.

The city's major daily newspaper put me, by virtue of owning a period car and a word-of-mouth referral, on the vintage automobile beat, sending me on expeditions to murky garages in Brooklyn's innards and to North Jersey junkyards and eventually on road trips to points farther afield. A journalist asked me to do background research for a book, innocently offering to pay me in wine. "As many bottles as you can fit into your trunk," he merrily told me over the phone. Both he and his wife were renowned wine critics and they had the stuff in spades. When he opened the front door of his home north of the city in Cheever country to greet me, I could see by his fixed smile that it hadn't occurred to him I might drive an American car built during the era when cars were known as boats. A Fairlane's trunk capacity compares favorably to the hold of a middle-sized shrimp trawler. Nonetheless, he was gracious about it and I drove back to the city on the New England Thruway cautiously, laden low by my new wine collection in the stern but buoyed by the knowledge that I wouldn't need to spend money on one of life's necessities for some time to come.

Intermittent gardening, periodic journalism, hebdomadal bartending, and the odd barter. It was an irregular living, but I reasoned that if Sunny, who hadn't drawn a regular paycheck since his tour of duty with the Air Force, had been able to cobble a life together all these years, so could I. That modeling oneself on Sunny's brand of bohemianism while living in one of the world's costlier cities was more likely to put a person on the path to penury than prosperity was a thought I left unexplored. Most midlife crises clear up on their own; mine would take root.

24

Francisco

"MOTHER OF THREE SLAIN BY A FIEND; BODY CUT IN Two. Killer Seized by Policeman as He Drops Severed Legs into East River"

A man gazed out sullenly from the page of old newsprint. His cheeks were bruised and his mouth was slack and his eyes defeated, like a fish on ice. It was a humble and sullen peasant face, a stony and unlucky villain. It was also Sunny's face.

I had never doubted the basic truth of anything Sunny told me. Which isn't to say that I always took him at his word. At worst, he was an exceptionally unreliable narrator (which has never been a character flaw in my opinion), remembering and misremembering events in his life with equal facility. At his best, he was a masterful confabulator who frequently ad-libbed his way through personal history, in order to cover up his lapses in memory, and general history, in order to make up for his limited formal education. I had figured this out long ago and so the proper names, the dates, the precise chronology of any story he told me mattered less than Sunny's vision of the event. Where he digressed from plausibility, he usually enriched the past. Each time he recounted the murder of the bar's iceman, for instance, it sounded less like an account of a real crime than an old-time radio detective drama. *I was a boy, how old I don't recall but I hadn't taken my first communion yet,* he might say. *I was asleep next to my brothers Peanuts and Brother when I was woken, not by my mother as usual, but by the backfire of a car. Or so I thought. I began to drift off to sleep again when I heard a growing commotion outside on the street and I got up and ran to the window and leaned out and saw a pool of red as if a bucket of paint had been kicked over and the body of a man laying on the stoop. A crowd of longshoremen stood around looking on while in back of a booth inside the store, a gun was wrapped in newspaper like a butcher steak waiting for my father to discover it. . . .*" Sunny's version was one part Weegee, two parts Hammett. He couldn't tell you the year, the motive, the names of the shooter or the victim, or why the crime took place here and not elsewhere on the delivery route, but such details hardly seemed to matter. Only those who didn't know him well talked to Sunny to come by information.

This made it all the more peculiar that it was at Sunny's request that I found myself in the microfilm room of the public library, scrolling through blurs of newsprint, in search of corroboration, and illumination, of an episode in family history that had been either forgotten, buried, or repressed.

The day before, he had invited me over for breakfast as he did from time to time and while he had stirred eggs in a skillet and kept an eye on coffee warming in a saucepan, he said over his shoulder and out of the blue, "You know, Timmy, standing here as I am, I have to think of how my mother's life might have been so different if *her* mother, my grandmother, had not caught on fire by the stove. In a sense, my mother never really got to have a mother. . . ."

Memories of working in her uncle's Coney Island wine bar as a teen had given Josephine the lifelong conviction that bars were no place for women, and the only sign she gave of her existence to the outside world was a near-imperceptible parting of the curtains, a pious window peeping at the comings and goings in the street below. Increasingly frail in her final years and in the end, bathed and changed and fed by Sunny, who came from a generation for whom nursing a parent was a filial, not a salaried, matter, she had died several winters earlier after taking a fall during the Christmas holidays. But Sunny still spent much of his time in her apartment, more comfortable amongst his mother's simple furnishings and godly knickknacks than in the disarray of an apartment shared with a young child. Fatherhood had been more wearying than he'd expected.

"Did your mother see her mother die?"

"I don't think she was in the room but if she was, she would have been very young. Too young to know what was happening, perhaps. But my mother did see a lot of bad shit and she had a lot of psychological problems later in life. She was always somewhat shy, somewhat quiet. Even when she was younger, I never knew her to go into the street to socialize with the other women. She had herself committed to a psychiatric hospital when I was in my twenties and perhaps several times after that, I am not really sure."

"I don't think you ever mentioned that to me."

"No, Timmy, I haven't. These things, it's best to let them

go, aye? But in this case, I haven't been able to. You see, what had happened, at some pernt when she was a child my mother suffered a trauma. She witnessed a body being chopped up."

He scraped the eggs onto two plates with fried potatoes and set them on the table and he sat down across from me. We ate in silence while I waited for Sunny to continue.

"I didn't know any of this when I was growing up. I didn't learn of it until I was a grown man when my mother came to visit me once at my loft on Wooster Street. My mother was never the type to get on a train and go to Manhattan. Manhattan might as well have been Chicago to her. But one day she showed up at my studio and it was like a miracle to see her. I hadn't been to Red Hook in quite a few years and I was so taken by the sight of her at my door. This little woman, my mother. I made us tea and she began to relate this event to me, this atrocity that had been hanging in her mind her entire life."

Sunny lowered his voice though we were alone.

"I trust your honor, your friendship," he said, haltingly. "I have never spoken to anyone about this other than my brother Ralph. Not Tone, not to my family, not to my friends. But I'm telling you so you might understand why my mother was the way she was. She must have been living with her aunt and uncle when this occurred. Anyway, she and her brother—my uncle Tony—went to visit their father one day. Perhaps they intended to surprise him because when they entered his apartment, there was a body there of a woman cut in two. What an experience that must have been for her. For any child. I don't know the details, but my grandfather was arrested for murder and apparently there was a trial and in the end, he was found innocent. Nonetheless, the stigma was so great that he changed his name, from Travia to Travis. Francisco Travia became Frank Travis. My mother never spoke of that incident again and I never knew all of what took place. I loved my grandfather very much, Timmy. He was always so kind to me and I've not been able to reconcile this bloody image with the man I knew.

"The truth of the matter is there is so much that I don't know and that I would like to know. And I know that you have some knowledge of these things, of how to look up old newspapers, police files, whatnot. I wonder whether in your spare time you might be able . . ."

"I can try to do that, Sunny."

"I would so very much appreciate that. Me, I wouldn't know where to start at a library, in that sea of words. I don't think I've read ten entire books in my life. I wish I had that capability."

He refilled our mugs with coffee. "My mom was a sweet lady, Timmy. I mean, really, really nice. Too bad she had to spend a good part of her life regurgitating those experiences that got to her very early on."

What to Sunny might have seemed an overwhelming endeavor had taken no more than several hours of sitting crosslegged on a library floor, combing the small print of heavy-bound volumes of annual newspaper indexes for the name Travia. Even so, the moment of discovery of a lone entry for *Travia, Francisco* had been unexpectedly affecting. While I had never sought validation of Sunny's memories, it had seemingly come to me nonetheless.

"Travia." The caption beneath the photograph of Sunny's grandfather misspelled his name as Francisco Trapia. I returned to the top of the page and began reading.

A middle-aged woman, a wife, and mother of three children, was beaten to death with a huge chisel and then hacked in two with a butcher's knife early today in a flat on the top floor of 56 Sackett St.

Her slayer, Francisco Trapia, aged 33, of the Sackett St. address, was captured by the police and under severe questioning he has told varying stories. He was caught trying to dispose of the legs he had severed from the body.

At first the police believed his tale that the woman was a waterfront character, known only as "Marie," but at noon the torso—all of her body that has been recovered—was identified at the morgue in Kings County Hospital as that of Mrs. Anna T. Frederick, 42, of 566 Henry St.

Husband Identifies Her

The identification was made by her husband, Frederick Frederick, who became prostrated at the Morgue and was unable to help the police much in determining how his wife had come to be in Trapia's clutches. He insisted that his wife was a good woman and that she was devoted to her children.

Ms. Frederick failed to come home at 6 o'clock last night, he said, but he did nothing about it until this noon when he sent their daughter, Anna, 13, to the Hamilton Ave. station to report her as missing. The police questioned the child and then sent for the father.

Sees Man Carrying Bundle

At 7 o'clock this morning Patrolman James Anderson of the Hamilton Ave. station was standing on post at India Wharf and Hamilton Avenue. He was soaked through from the heavy rain and fog and it was so murky that he could not see the tugs that were fog-horning their way through the adjacent waters.

Looking toward Hamilton Ave., he observed a phantomlike figure scurrying along, blurred in the mist. He looked closely, for the man appeared to be misshapen. Then Anderson observed that the fellow was carrying a bundle on his head. It was a queer bundle, of burlap and an old army overcoat. The man kept looking behind as he hurried toward the wharf.

Drops Bundle in Water

Patrolman Anderson started to intercept the man before he could reach the pier, but the man heard him and moved faster, darting ahead in quick spurts.

"Where you going there?"

The man heard the patrolman's shout and ran headlong, reaching the pier first and dropping, then kicking, his bundle over the edge into the thick, oily water. Then the man ran and Anderson went after him.

Over Conover St., up Hamilton Ave., over Van Brunt St., Anderson emptied his pistol in the air. He knew workmen were on their way to the piers at that hour and in the uncertain fog he didn't dare shoot directly at the fleeing figure. It was all he could do, in his heavy raincoat, to keep the man in sight.

Cop on Post Halts Him

A block from the Hamilton Ave. station Patrolman Louis Vitalo was standing on post. He heard the shots and looked and was almost bowled over by the figure catapulting out of the fog. He grabbed him and the two went down. Anderson came up quickly and it was all both policemen could do to subdue their prisoner.

At the Hamilton Ave. station Capt. Daniel O'Connor was just going on duty. Anderson turned in his prisoner.

"I don't know what it's all about, but there's something mighty funny," he said.

The prisoner gave a name and address. Detectives were dispatched to the place. No such person was known. He gave addresses at Coney Island and South Brooklyn. All proved false.

Taxi Driver Gives Clue

Then Captain O'Connor sent Anderson and Vitalo with Sgt. John Weisenrider down to India Wharf to see about the bundle. They ran into Rocco Zaquerella, a taxi driver, of 45 Sackett Street.

"I know that guy you was chasing this morning," said Zaquerella to Anderson. "He lives up

at 56 Sackett—Apartment 19. I was on my way
to the garage and I saw you leggin' it. His name
is Trapia."

The police went to No. 56. They broke into
the three-room flat on the top. In the first room,
they found nothing. In the second, they saw
where someone had been sleeping. It was dark
and they threw their searchlights on the floor.

In a bundle they found the nude torso of a
woman, crudely severed just above the hips. The
carpet was soaked in blood. On the floor was the
chisel—of steel with a large wooden handle.

Breaks Down, Admits Crime

The police hurried back to their station. Trapia
at first was sullenly indignant. Then he broke
down.

Captain O'Connor got an idea.

"Take off your shoes," he ordered.

Trapia did and disclosed blood-soaked woolen
socks.

"I killed her," he said.

Then he told of having known the woman for
ten months.

"Revenge" His Motive

Trapia said he killed her in revenge.

"Last night she come to my house. She was
drunk. She fell asleep. I couldn't sleep. So I get
up. I get the chisel. I hit her on the head," he confessed.

Acting Capt. George Bishop, in charge of detectives of the 11th district, notified Deputy Inspector John J. Sullivan, head of Brooklyn police, and both took a detailed statement from Trapia. By the time they finished with him, Trapia realized that he had said too much and he changed his story.

Calling Lieut. John Rand he gave another version. He said the woman came to his place and he told her to go away. But she sat down in a chair and he was going to pick her up and toss her out when he saw that she was dead.

That, according to his last story, was at 9 o'clock last night. A dead woman in his flat worried him. The idea of cutting her in two and throwing the pieces in the harbor struck him. No one would ever know, because no one ever inquired about "Marie."

He was charged with homicide and an autopsy will be performed tomorrow at King's County Hospital after the Marine police recover the legs from the water.

What I knew of Sunny's family had always been limited by the frailty of his memory. It was like standing in a kitchen and through a swinging pantry door, observing the Balzanos and the Travias seated around a dinner table in a room that was only lit by occasional flashes of lightning coming through a window. Now a lamp had abruptly been turned on above the head of one of the guests.

When I called to let Sunny know that I had succeeded in finding accounts of his grandfather's case, he invited me to come over straightaway.

"I'll fix us breakfast!" he said, though it was the afternoon. It was his favorite meal and he would prepare it any time of day and sometimes very late at night when a bartender's stomach is at its hollowest.

I pulled the articles out of my bag and placed them on his dining table. "I have to confess, I'm feeling anxious about learning what it is that you have uncovered," he said. Sunny put on his reading glasses and leaned over to look at the photograph of his grandfather.

"Wow. Amazing. I don't see him that way in my memory. Although I see my mother's features—I see the cheekbones— but he looks really bad. He's just a kid here. That's amazing. How old does it say he was here?"

"Thirty-three years."

"Thirty-three years old. My grandfather. I love you. My grandfather. I don't have any photographs of him, Timmy. I haven't seen his face except in my mind for fifty, sixty years." Sunny bit back tears.

"You don't see him as you remember him?" I asked quietly.

"I am beginning to now. He's got black hair and when I knew him, his hair was white. But the hairline is the same. I can cut through all of this and see the beautiful man that I knew. What's this say? 'Mother of three children. Slain by a friend, body cut in two'?"

"Fiend. 'Slain by a fiend.' You want me to read it to you?"

"Yeah. They probably cuss him out. They make him seem like a real piece of shit, I'm sure."

I read each of the stories aloud, including a *Brooklyn Eagle* story with the memorable headline "Woman Not Dead When Travia Cut Off Legs." Sunny listened raptly.

When I had finished, he let out a long sigh and held his grandfather's picture in front of him in silence. I began clearing the table.

"That's what my mother must have seen," he said after a while. "My mother must have been brought up into that apartment by her brother, my uncle Tony, and there was blood all over.

"I'd like to go to that address and the wharf, Timmy. The fact that they acquitted him after an hour of deliberation had to be the result of a very smart lawyer, because it seems to me that from what I just heard, I would have said, 'Hang the son of a bitch.' And they could have. That picture of him is really diabolical looking. In those days, if you were Italian you were guilty before you were proven innocent."

I told him his grandfather's lawyer was in fact Alfred E. Smith, the son and namesake of New York's most famous governor and head of the 1928 Democratic Presidential ticket. This was Smith's first case and he relied on the testimony of the chief medical examiner, Charles Norris, who convinced the jury that Ms. Frederick had died of carbon monoxide leaking from the stove after a coffeepot had boiled over and extinguished the pilot light. It was the first use of forensic pathology in a trial defense in American history and Norris would later say that the Travia case was the most notable of his career.

"Al Smith! This is all such a surprise to me, Timmy. I never imagined my family connected to his name, Timmy. And in such a way."

He stared at his grandfather's miserable face again.

"I was much closer with this grandfather than with my grandfather Balzano—who I lived with. Sometimes I think it's true that familiarity can breed a kind of contempt. The thing you miss most is the thing you're not with most of the time and I was hardly ever with Grandfather Travia. He was a mystery to me. He didn't speak any English really, he lived in Coney Island, he wore a cowboy suit, and he worked at the Steeplechase Park. They had a stage, like a little theater, and his job was to slap the men on the ass with a slapstick—it was like a paddle that clicked—and to blow up women's dresses with an air blower.

"Unlike my other grandfather, I truly loved my grandfather Travia. I didn't know him really outside the experiences I had with him in Coney Island and in my experiences, he was a loving man. I would have liked to get to know him better but a kid is never going to get to know a man. Every now and then, we would go see my grandfather at the Steeplechase, blowing up the women's dresses and sometimes smacking *them* on the ass. He would take us backstage and introduce us to the clowns and midgets and whatnot, so we had a real feeling of belonging, of being insiders, and a kid feels good about something like that. Knowing what I know now, that circus must have had a real dark side. It was a freak show of a kind, and you think of the stories these people had to tell. They all had to have stories. They had to have backgrounds some of which might have been so dark. You know the expression, birds of a feather flock together? To me, the Steeplechase was a good example of that. People who came together in that environment, they had something in common outside the parade of acrobats and animals and tricks and gymnastics and tightrope walking. But I wasn't aware of that side. A kid has to rely on the obvious things and from what I knew of him, what I saw of him, my grandfather had a great heart.

"He was always giving me little presents from his treasure hunting and at Easter, he would bring me chicks or a bunny rabbit, which I kept in coops in the backyard. I'll never forget this one particular animal. And I tell you this story so you understand how I came to feel so differently about my grandfathers. I had a lot of heartbreaks when it came to animals, even as a grown-up. The truth of the matter is I've suffered as great a pain from the loss of some of my animals as I have from my own family. Well, I had a bunny rabbit that Grandfather Francisco had given me and every morning before school, I would run downstairs and feed that bunny rabbit. I looked forward to seeing him. One day, the rabbit wasn't there. I remember it was on a Sunday because on Sundays, we would usually go to my grandmother's next door for dinner. So, I ran next door and up the stairs into the room where the whole family was sitting and I said, 'Grandpa, where's my bunny rabbit? I can't find my bunny rabbit!' And my grandfather Balzano and a good many of the folks at the table began to snicker. They couldn't answer the question but I could perceive what the situation was. The food on their table was my fuckin' bunny rabbit. How could anyone not feel some compassion for the pain of a child whose pet was on the dinner table? But that was my grandfather Balzano. And that was the beginning of my loss of any real sort of affection for him.

"Once that had taken place, I began to not treat him with the same kind of respect as I did before that happened. I became a grown-up of some kind after that, even though I was young.

"I am glad I got to know my grandfather Travia as I did. But I reflect sometimes, I watch the images in my memory and I imagine him bringing all these wonderful things to us and treating us as kindly as he did, and I imagine him up on that stage, in his cowboy suit. And then every once in a while I get this flash of him cutting up a body. It's a strange juxtaposition of images. The image where he's doing this thing, chopping up a body, that's my imagination. That's not a memory that comes from living and experience. But nonetheless, it's as powerful to me as though I had witnessed it.

"But, Timmy, thank you for doing what you did. You have to understand I truly loved my grandfather. He was a great guy. He ended up in a nursing home. He died by fire as well. Smoking in bed. Not only did his wife die by fire, he also died by fire.

"I still love him. I love him."

25

Christina's World

THE YEARS HAD BEEN GENEROUS TO SUNNY. HIS FACE was unmarked by wrinkles and although his hair had turned a streaked gray, it was as abundant as a child's—my own had been in recession since my twenties. He was also one of those people who seemed not to be aging so much as always coming of age. Ever idealistic, rarely cynical, he had the carefree, and occasionally imprudent, attitude of someone who believed that their whole life was ahead of them. Another man his age might begin planning for his golden years by, say, belatedly opening a retirement account; Sunny's 401K was a painting given to him one night by an elderly gangster, unsuspecting of its worth. Though unsigned, Sunny had a hunch—he was, after all, very familiar with Cubism—but he maintained a poker face until after he saw the man to the door, whereupon he quickly turned the lock and dimmed the lights should the man have a change of heart. He would go to some trouble to have it authenticated but wasn't both-

ered by the minor detail of provenance. Cervantes would
have made a case study of Sunny.

In drinking, he could still outlast any customer at the bar
and it seemed likely he would outlive many of them as well.
Though I never knew him to behave particularly drunkenly,
Sunny drank more than anyone I had ever known. He drank
when he worked with me on Friday nights but also in the
mornings afterward. He drank in the way people snack between meals and preferred drinking to eating—although over
six feet tall, he weighed little more than one hundred and
thirty pounds. A shot of whiskey was his idea of the perfect
interlude, and a cigarette the perfect conclusion not only to
the carnal but to every occasion.

A customer who commuted to Alaska to work on fishing
boats for part of the year observed once, "Sunny sure spends
a lot of time mallemaroking."

"Mallemaroking?" I said.

"It's a word with a very specific definition that is something like: 'the reveling and boozing of sailors whose ships
are frozen into the ice off the coast of Greenland.' We may
not be off the coast of Greenland and we may not be ice-
bound, but Sunny sure acts like we are. In fact, the man mal-
lemarokes year round."

More than once would it occur to me that the customer
base at Sunny's was unusually knowledgeable.

The first suggestion that Sunny's lifestyle was catching
up to him was the electric scooter that he received from Tone
as a present. It was the seated kind that is usually driven by
the infirm. He had been complaining about getting easily
winded after taking short walks or going up a flight of stairs;
a stroll to the pier at the end of the block had become a daunt-

ing hike. In the ensuing months, he could be seen periodically taking rides to the nearest bodega for cigarettes and other essentials. It may have been the only scooter in Kings County that had a cudgel concealed in the shopping basket that hung from its handlebars. Sunny had lived in Red Hook too long not to hold on to his old precautions.

One morning he woke not only short of breath but with an unfamiliar tingle below. It felt to him like athlete's foot . . . but of the penis. Soon his urine began turning dark with blood and his doctor, suspecting bladder cancer, scheduled a biopsy.

"It's so cold," Sunny said as he got in the car and wiped his wet hair from his face. "I feel like a dog pissing against a fire hydrant during an ice storm. While being yelled at!" It was a raw day, rain mixing with snow as we drove the length of Red Hook in the direction of the hospital.

"On my way over here," I said, "I was thinking there is a symmetry to the fact that we're going back to the same hospital where the nurse took your temperature—rectally, as I'm sure you recall—to have a camera inserted into your penis. You're getting it from both sides."

"A camera? Up my prick?"

By Sunny's shaky laugh I realized that Sunny hadn't given too much thought to how a biopsy of the bladder is performed and also that his usually cheerful disposition was sustained by the truism that it's often best not to know too much. Cancer had begun attacking my mother the year before and I had learned more about our fragility firsthand than I had ever wanted.

"Yes, Sunny. They call it a cystoscopy." I didn't possess

Sunny's insouciance and I had read up on the subject after
Sunny had called to tell me his doctor's suspicions.

"Goodness. Medicine has changed so much. I remember
I used to get nosebleeds as a child and in order to stop the
bleeding, my mother would hold a cold knife against the back
of my head. For earaches, she'd put bags of salt on the coal
stove. Or warm up olive oil and swab the inside of my ears
with her finger. People relied on themselves in those days. My
uncle Dominick—the one who raised my mother—he died of
blood poisoning from pulling his own tooth with pliers. And
if you got really sick, you had to rely on the gods."

After signing in, we began the long wait customary to
hospitals. Sunny asked me to join him downstairs for several
cigarette breaks. He smoked, I fretted. I was beginning to
have an inkling of just how bullheaded a patient he was going
to be. Along with the principle of carpe diem, impenitence
had always been his modus vivendi. I knew that this day
could still go either way—that Sunny was as apt to suddenly
say, "Take me home," as he was to submit to a surgeon's ether.
When his name was finally called, he gave the exit door one
deliberating look but took the gown and slippers obediently
from the nurse. Women had always had a great sway over
him.

We were alone in the changing room. Sunny sat down on
a bench and began undressing and I turned away to give him
some privacy and studied myself in a full-length mirror that
hung on the wall.

"I look young, Sunny. Not forty. I don't feel forty. And I
sure don't act forty."

"No, you don't, Timmy. Keep the enthusiasm. Stay well.

Stay a child for the old life." He grunted. "My feet get so cold. Here, help me with these slippers.

"Thank you, Timmy," Sunny said with pleasure. "Putting on a pair of socks can feel better than sex sometimes. You only got one prick, but you have ten toes."

"You've got a way with words," I said.

"And you with hands!"

I sat down on the bench next to him and Sunny caught sight of me looking at a scar descending from the hem of his hiked-up gown and running down his thigh to his knee.

"My gunshot wound. You might say it was the beginning of my notoriety."

"I thought the time you heisted a safe was the beginning of your notoriety."

"Nye. That was just the beginning of my disrepute. And mind you, the culprits of that crime were never apprehended."

"I see. Well, go on. I suspect there's more to it than your run-of-the-mill bullet wound as you never seem to do things in an ordinary way. Not even being shot."

"Ha. There's a lot of truth to that, Timmy. In fact, in this case, you might say I was my own quarry."

Suddenly I found myself hoping there would be further delays that afternoon. I was finally going to hear the rest of the story that Sunny had begun the night we went to see George Plimpton.

"It was 1956. I was discharged from the Air Force shortly before Thanksgiving of that year and I had moved into an apartment in San Bernardino. I was about to begin attending the American Academy of Dramatic Arts in Los Angeles. Everyone I knew had gone home for the weekend except my friend Butchie and we were feeling a little sorry for ourselves.

So we decided we would shoot a rabbit for our Thanksgiving meal. I was never much for guns, not even in the military, though as a boy I used to make zip guns from car aerials. Twenty-two caliber. Anyway, Butchie was able to borrow a pistol but as we're driving out to the desert I'm starting to think, 'I can't shoot a fuckin' bunny rabbit.' I was probably remembering the rabbits my grandfather used to bring me as a child. We were drinking some beers and when we get out there, I said to Butchie, 'Why don't you just throw some of these bottles in the air and I'll shoot those instead.' The gun was a single-action revolver, like you see in the old westerns— with a hammer that you have to cock with your free hand before each shot. And it came with a holster. The real McCoy."

Sunny stood up and went into a gunfighter's stance, his feet firmly planted in his fresh pair of no-slide slipper socks, his right hand hovering over an imaginary butt while his own flashed from the gap in his gown.

"Gary Cooper in *High Moon,* Sunny?"

"Ha! *High Moon.* I'll have to remember that one, Timmy, but actually, I was thinking *El Topo.* That's one of the greats. Well, by the time I manage to draw the gun out of the holster on my first try, the bottle had already fallen back to earth. So this time, I cock the hammer beforehand, you see." He pantomimed pulling the hammer back and carefully slipping a pistol into its holster, and then returned to a tense crouch, ready to gun down the next nurse who opened the door.

"Butchie throws another bottle in the air like he's releasing a fuckin' dove." Sunny pitched his left hand upward, acting out both parts now. "I slap my hand against my hip and . . . *Pow!*"

Sunny fell back on the bench, gripping his thigh as though he'd been shot all over again.

"The bullet tore right through my leg. I thought I was a goner, Timmy. There was so much blood. I don't know if it nicked an artery or what. Butchie got me up and helped me to the car and lay me in the backseat and drove me to the hospital and by the time we arrived, it looked like an animal had been slaughtered back there. He carried me out and left me on this grassy hill while he ran inside to get help. I don't know if you know the painting *Christina's World* by Andrew Wyeth?"

"I was one of those students that art history professors, all professors for that matter, prefer to forget. Distracted."

"Well, it's of a girl lying in a meadow and gazing up at this farmhouse. There's a real tranquility in that painting and when I first saw it later it reminded me of that feeling I had when I was lying in that grass. I could just feel my life draining out of me but I felt very much at peace. They were of course able to save me, and my leg. But I would develop gangrene afterward and need a vein graft and end up in a VA hospital here in Brooklyn. But the part of the story that really got me was the headline in the local newspaper the next day. It read: 'Man Outdraws Self.'"

Sunny roared.

"There I was! 'Man Outdraws Self.' I made the paper! I was *immortalized*. Well, by the time I got home to Brooklyn, I had such a limp from the infection, my mom treated me like a war hero. Meanwhile, I'm like the biggest fuckup there is. But as it turned out, shooting myself was the beginning of a real transformation for me. The doctors were so kindly and while I was recovering in that hospital they began bringing me art books. Books on Vermeer, Courbet, Rembrandt, Picasso. These doctors were some of the first authority figures who treated me with decency and encouraged my artistic ambitions. I ended up spending the better part of a year there and when I was released I took the train straight to Manhattan. I wasn't going back to Red Hook. I was going to be *an artist*."

We spent the entire afternoon in pre-surgery as the beds around us filled and emptied with patients. I read to myself and aloud to Sunny to pass the time, sensing that people wondered how the two of us were related. I was too old to be a grandson and I didn't have the eyes, nose, lips, or chin of a son. Various doctors and nurses and residents periodically came by to take his vital signs, insert an IV, pose questions, and fill out paperwork—any excuse, it seemed, to spend time with the patient whose chart said Antonio Balzano but who instructed everyone to please call him Sunny.

"Listen to what this writer says. A Nobel Prize winner, actually. From Mexico. 'Neither the phallus nor the ass have a sense of humor.' "

"Oh?"

" 'Being sullen, they are aggressive.' "

"You know that I don't read books, Timmy, and I can't really speak with authority to what it is that it is that this author is saying, but he must have had very limited experience in life. I mean what is more ridiculous—and diverting, I might add—than the prick and the ass?

"Look at what my prick is putting me through today. There had better be humor involved and the only way the mind can respond is with a sense of humor."

An anesthesiologist came over with a clipboard. "Do you

have any allergies?" she asked, and Sunny crinkled his brow as if in thought and replied with great seriousness, "Why, yes, I do. I don't seem to be able to take women's perfume any longer."

She smiled shyly and after she finished writing in his chart, she began rolling up his sleeve to take his blood pressure.

"I thank you," Sunny said.

"I'm not done yet," she replied.

"I thank you anyway," he said.

As she walked away, Sunny said to me, "Seeing Anastasia smile is like seeing a little piece of God."

"Her name's not Anastasia. It's Dina. Dina, the anesthesiologist. The way you muddle things is like a gift from God, Sunny."

There was no place and no situation where Sunny did not consider flirting to be the most suitable form of communication with a woman. Naturally he flirted with customers at the bar, but also with waitresses taking his order, with receptionists taking his name, with nuns casting him in their pageant, with nurses inserting catheters, and with anesthesiologists about to put him under. I had seen him flirt wordlessly and from great distances. While sitting in traffic once, I noticed how he looked across the street and gave a smile and a little wave to a young woman sitting by a window. She responded in kind. He often asked aloud, "Where would we be without women?"

To most women, there was an innocence to his flirting since he was usually one, and often two, generations older than they. To Sunny innocence was the very point of flirting. He was in love with falling in love and he would sometimes say, "The dance can be beautiful but just don't get into the ring, Timmy."

"It's funny how all these memories become buoyant and bob on your consciousness," Sunny said after a while. "You catch them before they sink again."

"What's bobbing on your consciousness now, Sunny?" I asked.

"Well, I've been thinking about what you said earlier how you're not really feeling your age. I don't know whether I told you of this experience I had not so long ago with my friend from childhood, George Hunt?"

"The one who talked you into joining the Air Force?"

"Yes. Matter of fact, I wouldn't have shot myself if it hadn't been for him just like I wouldn't have nearly drowned if it hadn't been for you.

"Anyway, there was a knock on the door of the bar and when I opened it, there was an old man standing there and he said to me, 'You know who I am?' I peered at him and I really couldn't figure out who he was. But there had been a girl who'd lived around the corner when I was a kid, Patricia Esposito. And my friend George Hunt had married her. And I saw Patricia Esposito standing behind this old man. So I said, 'You're George Hunt!' I hadn't seen him in over fifty years. My best friend from when we were kids, you understand. I invited them inside and we sat at the first booth in the bar and it was strange—I looked at him and I was able to reach into the structure of his face, but his spirit was gone. He was not at all like the George Hunt I knew. He was dead. He was alive but he was dead. I can feel him now saying, 'Sunny, don't say that.' But he was. I asked him if he would like a drink and he said, 'I can't drink.' We had a short conversation. We never said anything about the past. It was almost like the past didn't exist. And I know he didn't want to regard the past because he had a hell of time with it, too. His father had died when he was young and his mother got married again—to this little guy, this near-midget Lip-Lip Leo that everyone made fun of. That the kids threw rocks at. To be the son of Lip-Lip Leo's wife, you wanted to crawl in a hole. It broke George's heart. And not long after that visit, I received another visit—this time from George's sister who came with her husband and I sat with them and talked for an hour. In my mind I said to myself, 'My goodness, all these people that it is that I'm meeting from those days—they're like old people. Am I that old?' In my mind I said it would have been a good thing not to ever see them again because I was holding these memories in my imagination. I remembered George as a child, a teen-ager full of passion, and his sister as being very sexy, very beautiful. And now I'm seeing them and they're old and the only thing that hasn't changed is me. I don't feel old. I guess I am old but I don't and did not regard myself as being in the same place they were. It was not too long thereafter that I heard George had passed away. I regard that reality now and I regard the memory of what it was like in the early days when we were all young and enthusiastic and possessed all these dreams as to what we were about to do—embark on life. And I feel very blessed because I'm still embarking, aye? And all these other things I've held in my imagination have fallen to the quest of the reality of life. And that's good. This moment is real. This moment is sweet. I have this."

In the late afternoon, Dina, the anesthesiologist, returned and told him that he would be going into surgery shortly. Sunny said, "Timmy, I wonder if you could hold these for me?" He reached into his mouth and took out his teeth and handed them to me. His face caved and he looked at me with embarrassment and I felt a surge of pity. He had always hated the inauthentic. I promised that I would bring them to him as soon as he woke up and I was allowed into the post-op room. "Thank you, Timmy," he mumbled. "I love you, you hear?"

Dina took one hand to walk him to the operating room and with the other he held on to his IV drip pole and as the two slowly shuffled away, he turned to look at me over his shoulder. He didn't have to say it. What a candy store life can be.

26

Exposition Fermée

THE COWBELL ABOVE THE DOOR CLANGED AS I ENTERED Ferdinando's and the mayor of New York looked up from his spaghetti. He was seated at my regular center table, along with the police commissioner and their two consorts. I glanced at Frank and said, "It's all right, Frank. We'll sit somewhere else." He grinned and spread his hands as if to say, "Whaddyagonnado." I had continued coming here weekly for a decade now, mostly alone after my friends moved on. Once, Frank squeezed my shoulder from behind mid-bite and said, "Teem. You's like the captain that stays on the sinking ship. Loyal, know what I mean?"

On this night however, I had arrived with old friends in tow. Ferdinando's was nearly empty as usual and we sat down two tables over from the mayor. As his party was finishing their meals, he stood up and began making small talk with the only other customers, three middle-aged married couples sitting alongside us. I had been mulling over whether to invite him to Sunny's for a drink when the mayor leaned in close to one of the husbands. "Do you know what the secret to a successful marriage is?" he asked.

The man shrugged.

"Make your wife think she's getting laid when she's really getting fucked!"

Sunny had always maintained that it only takes "one fuckin' banana" in a bar to spoil it for everyone else. After we paid our bills, the mayor and I went our separate ways.

As I drove down Van Brunt Street, thinking to myself that the sight of the billionaire monarch of New York having dinner in Red Hook was an omen of sorts, I passed a celebrated French restaurant that had opened next to a funeral home. High cuisine in a low-rent neighborhood is its own passport to success in New York. A few blocks farther, just past a retro-nautical diner, silhouettes peered into Red Hook's newest liquor store, the first in memory where the goods were displayed conceptually—the gin laid out in a claw-foot tub—rather than precautionarily (behind bullet-proof glass) as is custom in the city's dodgier precincts. The store, named after its Alabaman owner, was already renowned far beyond the borders of Brooklyn for its exhaustive selection of whiskeys and bitters. The words "small-batch bourbon" and "artisanal bitters" should strike fear into the heart of any urban preservationist and they struck fear into mine. Admittedly, I was not so much a preservationist as a reservationist—I had reservations about anything that might help transform the desolation of Red Hook into a neighborhood resembling its northern cousins, Greenpoint and Williamsburg, once-run-down industrial areas that had lately been revived into something called *nouveau grit*.

———

SUNNY HAD EMERGED from surgery lightened of a cancerous mass and with the characteristic conviction of the chastened. He said that henceforth he would rein in his unhealthiest habits. His shortness of breath had been diagnosed as chronic obstructive pulmonary disease, which was a longer way of saying he had smoker's lung, and when he was told that he would have to give up cigarettes and hard liquor he took a shallow breath and nodded his agreement. But asking Sunny to forgo tobacco and whiskey was like calling on Lou Piniella to renounce temper tantrums. Just as every umpire once knew that despite expressions of contrition and pledges of reform, it wouldn't be long before Mr. Piniella would be throwing first base into the outfield and kicking dirt on their shoes again, everyone acquainted with Sunny's knew that smoking and drinking were inseparable extensions of his personality, not so much second nature as first.

Sunny tried for a while. He began taking vitamins and eating the occasional vegetable. He avoided the bar even when it was closed and spent ever more time in his mother's old apartment on the top floor while Tone and Oda remained downstairs. He said that he needed privacy and quiet to recover his strength but he confessed what he needed most were the two breath-stealing flights of stairs as a deterrent from temptation.

It was the first leave that Sunny took from the bar in anyone's memory. In the years since their daughter had been born, he and Tone had taken turns looking after her when the bar was open for business. Now Tone came in every open night. I had always thought that there were very few women who could get involved with Sunny without forever feeling overshadowed by his big personality and the devotion he received seemingly wherever he went. But, in his absence, she proved to be something of a Martha Gellhorn, who said of her marriage to Ernest Hemingway, "Why should I be a footnote in someone else's life?" Tone was determined to put her own stamp on the bar.

It had always galled her when customers referred to Sunny's as a dive and she soon ordered a pristine awning with *Sunny's Bar* printed on it. She converted the back room once used by mob conferees into an art gallery and the site of a weekly bluegrass jam and a knitting circle (Uncle John's subterranean neighbors at the cemetery surely detected a shift in the earth when word of this got out). She created an events calendar and a mailing list, and when a travel guide included Sunny's in their guidebook to New York, she placed their sticker prominently in the window. Always good with tools, she installed and secured and refurbished. She was well-intentioned in her industriousness. Quite unlike Sunny, it was her nature to keep busy and to always look for ways to improve on things. As one customer observed with a note of sadness, "Tone has vision."

Sunny kept to himself for most of a year. He occupied himself with drawing and watching television and plotting means to come by occasional cigarettes behind Tone's back. When he succeeded, he tucked them away in ones and twos on door lintels, well above her sight line. After he discovered an actor that he admired even more than Marlon Brando, he and Oda tuned in faithfully every afternoon to watch Sponge-Bob SquarePants's escapades. He was a very devoted father, though the relationship he formed with his daughter was one of equals rather than a paternal one. Indeed, after she had seen a popular pirate movie, Oda began referring to him not as Papa but as Captain Jack Sparrow. The resemblance was more than passing.

When Sunny did return to the bar, he returned unhumbled. Overconfident with a renewed feeling of well-being, he lit cigarettes and poured himself shots with the abandon of a mountain hermit who had a change of heart, descended to the nearest village, and set foot into the first tavern he came across. It was the beginning of a series of boom and bust cycles for him, in which each valley would be deeper than the previous one. He could be an exasperating person to try and reason with. The arguments of causation had no effect; in fact, he turned them on their head. If I gave him a reproachful look or merely said, "Sunny, please . . ." as he waited for me to refill his glass, he would irritably reply, "Timmy, it's living not dying that's going to kill me." He indulged himself in slow-motion benders until his breath gave out and he disappeared upstairs for weeks, months, and eventually entire seasons to convalesce. When people traveled to Red Hook expecting to find Sunny and learned that he would not be in that night, they were visibly crestfallen. I knew how they felt.

When I was twelve, I often walked after school to a rundown zoo at the edge of the African city where I lived. It was a somewhat perilous trip, taking me through less familiar neighborhoods and eventually on a dirt path through a shrubby forest. There were few animals in the zoo and they were poorly cared for, but I came for the lone lion that lived there. Its home was a simple cage like those in old traveling circuses and when the lion wasn't asleep it would pace restlessly back and forth. I had read the book *Born Free* by Joy

Adamson that year and on my walks home I would daydream about breaking the lion out. One day I arrived to find the cage empty and a sign that read, *Exposition Fermée.*

The man who took Sunny's absence the hardest was Casey, the lachrymose mobster who had first come to the bar as a teenage longshoreman. He had moved away, to a warmer city by the water, and with each return visit, the Red Hook he had known since he was a teenager was a little less recognizable. Amongst the bright facades of new stores and the fresh faces wearing modish clothes, he was suddenly the stranger in the strange land. Not finding Sunny behind the bar only seemed to deepen his disorientation.

He was often reckless when he appeared, parking his late-model car facing the wrong way or stretched across the sidewalk, throwing me the keys when I suggested moving it so as not to draw the attention of the police. And he was a mess—not from drinking, but from thinking. He was by turns in love and lovelorn, both states aroused by the same, much younger woman. He had begun to believe in retribution, not in the day-to-day variety that he may have dealt in at times, but one handed out by the cosmos. After his son had died suddenly in his sleep a few years earlier, he became consumed with the belief this was a rebalancing for some of the wrongs he had done in his life.

The last time I would ever see him, he sat on a stool at the deep end of the bar, his ruddy color now swallowed up by a deep tan, and he began talking drunkenly to a young couple visiting from out of town. As I sliced limes on the cutting board, I overheard snatches of the stories he was telling. Of hijackings, of robberies, of the impunity he and his crew had once enjoyed in the neighborhood to conduct their business.

He told them of the time when, in the middle of the day in the middle of Van Brunt Street, he gunned down the boom box of a drug buyer after the man had refused to turn down the volume. When the couple told him they were from Texas, he said he had been there on a weekend business trip once with a friend and by the time they left the population of Texas had been reduced by one.

I searched the faces of the couple and decided that they weren't entirely convinced this thickset blowhard wasn't embellishing his exploits. Nevertheless, I didn't want him to say something he might later regret and I came around the bar in the hope he would turn his attention to me. I poured us two shots and he pulled out his cellphone and showed me pictures of his girlfriend in her bikini. I cautiously complimented her. He told me that he should be happy—the sunny weather, the girl—but that he often drove his car aimlessly around this new home in tears. He said he was tired of the life he had lived since he was a boy and remorseful for his deeds, and that he wanted to do something else with the time he had left but didn't know where to begin. Though a nonbeliever, I prayed then for Sunny to appear. But I was left to my own devices to console the gloomy hit man. I told him that it wasn't too late to start over. "Casey, how do you see your life ten years from now?"

He looked at me morosely. "A lot of violence," he said.

As the hours wore on, his eyes became redder and his mood bluer and I suggested he might feel better if he went home but he gave me an abject look and muttered, "I don't got no home no more. I got no place."

Dawn eventually broke on the night and the darkness in which we had been sitting and he turned to the incoming light and said in a voice first surprised and then despondent, "The sun? The fuckin' sun."

He was unmoored.

He was Martha, the last passenger pigeon.

He needed Sunny's counsel.

A friend finally arrived from Staten Island to pick him up—a giant and gentle man named Bartholomew, in an orange polo shirt that hung to his knees (a goodfella emeritus, as I was later made to understand)—and after I had seen them to the door and begun to wipe down the counter, the phone in the bar rang as it often did around this time. Sunny was a fitful sleeper and when he would wake in the early morning he liked to call downstairs to ask me how the night had been. The phone line was terrible and always full of static, as if he was making a transatlantic call from the distant past instead of calling from two floors above, but I found the sound of his disembodied voice comforting. The loneliest hour in a bar begins after closing time. I told him that Casey had been in and that he was in an unusually despondent state of mind, even for him.

"It hurts me to know Casey's hurting, Timmy." his voice heavy with sleep. "He's been a real good friend to me over time. I could always count on him to come by if I was anticipating there was going to be some kind of trouble. He carried himself in such a way that merely mentioning that I was expecting him later at the bar would persuade any troublemakers to go find someplace else. To him loyalty has never just been a word, aye? He really worked hard to have this woman reciprocate his very strong affection for her, Timmy, and I was hoping that would serve to make him happy. But you know what? If you're not feeling good about yourself, a new relationship may do something for a while but you're still left with the essence of your person and that will always show its face."

I would often think over the years that Sunny never reached his full potential. Without training, other than his life experience, his insight into the psychologies of people was often profound. I never did see Casey again, though the last I would hear of him, he was still out taking drives alone in his palm-lined sunny paradise.

27

Disappearances

I OVERHEARD TWO ORTHODOX JEWISH MEN TALKING ON
the subway. One said to the other, first in what I took to
be Yiddish and then in English, "Days crawl, years fly." The
words echoed in my mind for months. By then it had been
well more than a decade since a series of random turns on a
solitary drive had led me to a career as an accidental bartender. The title itself was a misnomer since I had assiduously
remained, as George Plimpton would have said, a professional amateur, discreetly thumbing through a cocktail book
when faced with such complexities as Sidecars or Tom Col-
linses. Whether one could rightfully call a four-nights-a
month job a career was probably also questionable. I had
never become convinced that opening the bar on any other
night but Friday wasn't a mistake and I passed up additional
shifts, stubbornly holding on to the view that the only safe-
guard against routine—in life and in love—was infrequency. I
could be uncompromising to a perverse degree.

I had now been with Sunny three times longer than the years I spent in college—which at the time had seemed like a very pleasant eternity. My Manhattan job was a short-lived stint by comparison and my longest romantic relationship, too, had given way. The lone avid baseball fan that I ever met at Sunny's once compared my longevity to that of the three most steadfast Yankees—Jeter, Rivera, and Posada. "All of you came up in '95, which turned out to be a superb rookie class," he said. The dark side of constancy was the faint fear that, after years of watching customers come and go— moving on eventually to other pastimes, other cities, or, with parenthood, other priorities—I was being left behind. The progress of others, whether upward or just onward, always seems to remind me of my own rootedness. And after the *Queen Mary II* began berthing in Red Hook, the ship's ghostly passes just offshore seemed to carry with them a subliminal message. There is nothing like the sight of the world's largest ocean liner setting sail to make one feel unaccountably restless.

Unbeknownst to Sunny, I had made a private pact that I would stay as long as he lived. It was the sort of pledge one usually makes out of excessive self-regard—we all have illusions at various times of being indispensable in some province of our lives—but in this case, my motives were not altruism alone. I didn't want to miss a single thing Sunny said. How often can one say this of another person? He was the first person I knew whose company never became tiresome, his stories, even on their umpteenth retelling, never stale. But life has a habit of not cooperating with our plans. Sunny was slipping from existence into memory in his own lifetime. More and more often, late arrivals to Red Hook didn't know Sunny as a flesh-and-blood person but as a mysterious personage who was said to live in the top-floor room whose window light burned all night. Some customers didn't know anything about him at all, assuming that like John McSorley or P. J. Clarke or Ludwig Bemelmans, he was an entirely historical figure after whom the bar had been named.

Sunny and Sunny's had always been inseparable—I couldn't picture one without picturing the other, just as I couldn't devote myself to one without devoting myself to the other. That this would not always be so seemed impossible to me. The only truly indispensable person at Sunny's was Sunny. But the impossible was coming to pass. Like the headless horse on the wall and the nameless sailor in the window whose face was becoming more indistinct with each year, Sunny was fading as a presence in the bar and it seemed that not even his larger-than-life persona was able to slow the process.

With appearances on Friday increasingly rare, Sunny's periodic appointments with his urologist had become one of the few occasions we saw each other in person. Although having a camera eased up one's penis is not most men's idea of a good time—no matter how microscopic they make these things nowadays—and the waiting room was the kind of place where the fake flowers were wilting and Maury Povich was in the middle distance, forever appalled by someone's moral shortcoming, Sunny was never outwardly glum during these visits. He mostly accepted the indignities of the urological scrutiny to which he was subjected with his usual cheeriness, and I did my best to support him in this by pointing out the bright side of the situation whenever I found one. When I suggested that he was a very fortunate man to have his privates handled by such attractive nurses, he replied, "Timmy, I've had so many folks touch me in so many places I don't have any private ones left!"

Sunny treated all rooms as places to form friendships. I had accompanied Sunny to traffic court once and after the case was heard and dismissed, he presented the judge with a Cubist portrait he had made of him during the hearing, and on the way out, he surprised the bailiff with a paper airplane, saying to her, "May this give you flight to grander places." He was, of course, exceedingly popular with the hospital staff.

During one appointment he explained to his urologist and the head nurse that while he owned a saloon, he was also a painter and that to show his gratitude for the attention they gave him, he would like to make several paintings for the waiting room. Remembering the hidden penises in Sunny's paintings in the bar, I thought this was a sublime idea. His doctor was Slovenian and the nurses mostly Eastern European and they had the respect for the fine arts typical of those countries. Regrettably, he never got around to them, but Sunny was like that. He was forever making plans for the future. He had all the time in the world.

Although there had always been something eternal about Sunny, in the sense that he would be at home in any century, the inevitability of his physical mortality was brought home to me one Sunday. It was winter, the time of year when his lungs were most vulnerable. He had been taken to the hospital by ambulance after struggling for breath. I relieved Tone—she had a daughter to return to—and found him in the emergency room, his eyes wide behind a respirator mask. I squeezed his hand as he gave me a muffled greeting. Those whom we love will always look out of place lying in a hospital bed, the clinical setting such a contrast to their being as we know them. Many of the other patients were prisoners and were handcuffed to their beds, and the smell of the room was, at times, blinding. But to Sunny it was a matter of course to be gracious in ungracious circumstances. He asked that I write down the names of each orderly and each nurse that attended to him so that he could thank them in a more personal way. The afternoon turned into evening and the evening into night while we waited in the emergency room for a bed to open up. From the neighboring cot, a woman who had been beaten with a chair by her husband and who was illiterate asked whether she could dictate a letter for her social worker to me. "I'd rather live on the subway than go back home," I wrote for her. A policeman led in a teenager and shackled him to a chair nearby. He had drunk an entire bottle of vodka, though whether he had done so before or after inscribing the word "anarchy" with a black marker on his pant leg, I never learned. Sunny smiled at him with a look of understanding.

It wasn't until after midnight that a spot in a semi-private room became available. In the other bed lay an ancient black man who had lost his mind. He had no family and he cried and whimpered in his sleep. A nurse had turned his bedside television loudly to MTV's *The Real World,* which seemed like a cruel joke. The only reality was the one in this room.

It helped Sunny with his lungs to sit upright. I slumped in a chair and soon drifted off, waking up intermittently to Sunny gazing at me from behind his mask.

"That's strange. My fingernails look like the wings of a squid."

I opened my eyes again. Sunny was studying his hands.

"I wonder what's happening to me."

Though he had been awake since Friday, I realized that he wasn't going to fall asleep in the propped-up position he was in and I sat up, too, to give him company.

"I'm not sure there is a marine biologist on call on a Sunday night," I said. "But I'll buzz the nurse if you begin to change colors."

"Tell her to bring some lemon wedges," Sunny said, grinning a little.

"I've been thinking," he resumed in a croaky voice after a while. "I don't think I ever told you, but my father was brought here right before he died. He never went home again. He had the same thing they say I have. COPD. As did my brother Frank. I came here to see my father. He could barely speak. I fed him his last meal, a teaspoon of coffee. He couldn't get it down really, but I'll never forget his eyes as he looked at me. They were so grateful. He died with his hand in mine. My father was a wonderful man, Timmy, as was my brother. Brother would tell you stories. But never bullshit. He didn't know bullshit. A lot of the guys who he hung out with were Irish and Frank could sing every Irish song there ever was. He'd sing 'Danny Boy' and you'd cry because he sang it with such depth of feeling and he sang it better than the Irish guys, aye? I think of what the two of them had to go through.

"Brother challenged my father once when he was going through one of the really intense periods of his life. He must have been fifteen, sixteen. My father never raised a hand to any of us. If you were doing something that it was that wasn't right, he would pernt and you knew, you just didn't do it. We all had a great love and great respect for my father. We never feared him and we never wanted to hurt him either. But Frank challenged my father until he was left with no alternative but to say, 'You want to challenge me? You want to fight me?' And he took off his jacket. And my brother, he responded with, 'Yeah, I wanna fight you.' My father beat him badly. It was the darkest day of my life. The darkest day of all of our lives. How could this happen? I don't think we spoke to each other—anyone—for a month. It was like the house was full of clouds. But Frank did go to my father and he apologized and my father embraced him and he expressed how painful it was for him to have done what he had to do. He said, 'It wasn't for me, it was for you.' And my brother never went back to the life that he was getting involved in at that time."

"Right now my ability to access the past is so magnificently poignant, Timmy. Probably because I haven't slept for days. It's not like I'm telling the story of yesterday but of today."

He fell silent. The gums of the old man in the other bed flapped with his every exhalation. With whatever consciousness he had left, he might have concluded that he had arrived in the underworld as the denizens of *The Real World* mercilessly yammered on by his bedside. Outside the window, lights in Brooklyn Heights, the stirrings of early risers, were turning on one by one. The sight of common life resuming was comforting after a long night.

"We'll get you out of here, Sunny."

"I know, Timmy. You didn't pull me up out of the river so I could die one day in a place like this. I wonder if you could find me some coffee? My lips are so dry."

I went down to the street and I found a coffee-and-donut cart setting up for the day on the same corner from which

Sunny and I had once waved at cabs in our hospital gowns. Given time, it seems that one finds oneself standing in the same spot in Brooklyn at least twice in one's life (lending credibility to the idea we are following paths preset by celestial geometrists). When I returned, Sunny's eyes were closed, his hair draped to either side of him over his pillow. In profile, he looked like one of those incorrupt bodies of Italian saints encased in glass over whose face a prankster had slipped an oxygen mask. But he was only feigning death, breathing deeply, finally asleep, his beautiful mind perhaps conjuring houses full of clouds, perhaps summoning to life the gone. This wouldn't be my friend's last coffee.

28

Sometimes a Great Notion

It is not down in any map; true places never are.
—HERMAN MELVILLE

LIVE LONG ENOUGH IN NEW YORK AND EVERYONE tends to develop a theory as to when New York stopped being "New York." This is strictly a local phenomenon. No citizen of Boston, Wichita, or Seattle has ever bothered with this sort of municipal introspection, while in New York it is compulsory to periodically rhapsodize about the days when the city was more elegant, more seedy, more avant-garde, more soulful, more disreputable, more sophisticated, more freaky, more tolerant, more incomparable. This theory has its sub-theories, one for every neighborhood.

My oldest brother, Peter, tells a story. In 1979, he was a

young paralegal living in an apartment over an East Village bar named after its owner, Slugger Ann, a retired wrestler and the grandmother of Jackie Curtis, the drag queen performer and member of Andy Warhol's inner circle. My brother only knew Jackie Curtis by sight, but one morning as Peter was leaving for his job in midtown, Curtis approached him and asked whether he was going to be anywhere near the Pierre Hotel. Peter confirmed that he was. Jackie Curtis explained that he was working on an Audrey Hepburn act and that he very much needed to meet the actress to study her mannerisms in person. She was said to be staying at the Pierre and Curtis wondered whether my brother would do him the favor of delivering a note and a bouquet of flowers to her? Peter agreed and Curtis handed him twenty dollars. During his lunch hour, my brother picked up some white roses at a midtown florist and walked them to the Pierre. For my brother, the storied East Village was a place where a Warhol Superstar could hand a stranger twenty dollars and trust him to deliver flowers to an Audrey Hepburn.

(Lou Reed told another Curtis story: "Jackie is just speeding away. Thought she was James Dean for a day. Then I guess she had to crash. Valium would have helped that bash.")

For me, the decline of Red Hook began when newspaper and magazine articles began to regularly announce the rebirth of Red Hook. Such pronouncements are the kiss of death to certain kinds of neighborhoods. It wasn't long before sightseers and Sunday strollers trickled in like a nonnative species expanding into a once-inhospitable habitat and property speculators began to materialize as if confirming Aristotle's theory of spontaneous generation. In every dilapidated house and

grassy lot, they visualized the future condominium of mon-
eyed tenants colonizing a frontier neighborhood.

Sunny's daydreams of riding through Red Hook in his
white Central Park horse carriage were now being routinely
interrupted by the rumble of cars delivering a steady stream
of shoppers to the gourmet supermarket that had moved into
the abandoned Reconstruction-era warehouse at the end of
his block. The store's generator, erected steps from the bar,
hummed ceaselessly, and streetlamps blazed their mercury
vapors all night long over newly paved parking lots along the
water, obscuring the harbor from view.

Soon a developer would raise for scrap Red Hook's last
sunken wreck, *Lightship No. 84*, a decommissioned Coast
Guard ship that had been tied up and abandoned alongside
the pier of the defunct Revere Sugar Refinery until taking on
water some years earlier, leaving visible only two masts. It
had served as a romantic port of call or an observation post,
depending whether one was a bartender on an outing in the
bar's boat or a double-crested cormorant.

The sugar refinery's rusty cone-shaped dome, a structure
older than the Empire State Building and, at least in Red
Hook, just as iconic, was unceremoniously razed before anyone could say, "Wait just a moment." For a time the waterside
site was rumored to be the future home of a BJ's, a term
Sunny had always believed only applied to an activity more
numinous than discount shopping.

Down the block, the 140-year-old Todd Shipyard, whose
bright red-bricked walls I had encountered on my first drive
into Red Hook, rising up sharply from the curb of Beard
Street like the walls of a man-made canyon, was torn down
and its graving dock, once repair shop to the great ships, filled

in to make way for a megastore as impermanent-looking as the Scandinavian furniture that would be sold within. Outdoor speakers now broadcast European pop melodies in the dead of night to lost animals and lost souls, as well as the occasional bartender bicycling home from work.

Walk around Manhattan or any other metropolis and occasionally you will come across the sight of a single building, no more than two or three stories high, wedged incongruously between newer high-rise apartments or office towers. The entire block might be taken up by modern construction many stories tall except for a lone limestone row house or a humble wood-frame cottage, absurdly dwarfed, whose owner refused all offers. In architectural lingo, these curiosities have their own name: "holdouts." (In China, I was once told, these sorts of houses exist as well. They are given the more poetic name "nail houses," their owners being as stubborn as old nails that refuse to be dislodged.)

I was a holdout, too. It wasn't property but a memory and a love for a place that I wouldn't part with. There is nothing very useful about a sunken wreck, a retired shipyard, a crooked paving stone, or an untraveled street. They are no more productive than the Parachute Jump in Coney Island or the Pepsi-Cola and Citgo signs on the banks of the East and Charles Rivers. We are drawn to the window nonetheless, for these things color the view. As Sunny said after watching a smokestack being dismantled day by day, "These places are the personality of Red Hook. They've accumulated over time in just this way. Getting rid of them is like going to the doctor after you've lived most of your life and erasing the features that make each of us who it is that it is we are."

New York was, of course, only doing what cities always

do—moving ahead. But like any committed holdout in good standing, I tried to carry on as if nothing had changed at all. I ate my weekly meals at the same two-seater front table at Ferdinando's and drove straight through to Sunny's afterward, never setting foot in any of the latest bars, shops, or restaurants and looking stonily past every upmarket condo going up. I was something of an ornery type, better than most at nurturing a state of denial.

On a Wednesday night one December, an original harbor swimmer was in town, back from the Far West where he had moved some years ago. He wanted to see Red Hook and Sunny's one more time, he said. It was intensely cold and a fine snow was falling. I drove us along what had been our favored route when we first began coming here, what in a more rural setting would be the equivalent of taking the back roads. Past the Hess fuel tanks, the ball fields, and the silhouette of the old grain terminal and down teeth-jarring Beard Street where the shipyard buildings had stood. My friend asked to be let out a quarter mile from the bar so he could walk the rest of the way. He looked around in amazement at the newly flattened landscape and shouted, "Goddamn, it's all changed! All utterly changed." I left him behind and, by habit, drove slowly the rest of the way though the wild dogs that had patrolled this street had also disappeared, hopefully to kinder lots. A steady wind blew off the water. The bar sign creaked and the awning crackled overhead as we entered. We ordered boilermakers from Francis, though we had both stopped drinking them long ago. Behind him, a crockpot of cider burbled, releasing a billow of spiced steam whenever he opened the lid. A man named Charlie was playing a fiddle and a man named Bob a pedal steel guitar and a man named Andy a small drum set and a man named Smokey a Gretsch. They all wore ten-gallon hats, embroidered western shirts, and kerchiefs and they sang "You're Bound to Look Like a Monkey When You Grow Old" and "The Gold Rush is Over" and "The Sheik of Araby" and several dreamy girls stood alongside and mouthed the words and the moment might only have been improved upon if a figurine of Rudolph Valentino, the original Sheik, had been listening in from the shadows above. It was one of those splendid nights that Sunny's had perfected—sounds, sights, smells, and whiskey's sorcery blending to bring about a high degree of contentedness in the populace. Yet, a restlessness soon came over us. Perhaps it was the vanished buildings, the vanished stones, and Sunny vanished, too, upstairs, convalescing once again and listening to the overnight BBC as he now liked to do, but there was an underlying sense of disappointment to this reunion, like returning to one's alma mater and feeling a visitor, everything less familiar than one remembered. More levelheaded people than us might have foreseen this—homecomings have been prone to letdown at least since Odysseus's time.

"Let's get lost," I said.

We left our drinks behind and walked outside and made our way to the wooden pier behind the warehouse by which we used to climb down to the waterline. The pier had collapsed in places, leaving ominous gaps in the planks. Below, the water was rushing past, a conveyor belt to swift oblivion—too dicey even for nostalgic gamblers. "This way," I said. We took a path I knew to a nearby inlet where the current couldn't carry one away and we stripped and for a moment stood naked on the shore. It was very dark and the sky was low and the air full of snow. A curtain of inexhaustible flakes draped to the water. Somewhere there was a city. A statue. Another shoreline, perhaps with others, counterparts of ours, gazing at the same sight in reverse. All was obscured. There are passing visions that always remain, our private museum of images. A father swimming at dusk, a breast unveiled for the first time, a car burning bright in the night, a shoreline ringed with snow and us part of this vision, too. It was too cold to linger on these or any thoughts for long. We dove beneath the water and for a few silent moments, we were once again swimming headlong into the unknown, ecstatic boys in the Mississippi-Hudson River, invisible men moving through the lower depths.

ON SHORE, WE dressed quickly and hurried back to the bar, skin still wet, our faith in our invincibility and our own derring-do momentarily fortified. "We still got it!" Left unsaid that night (because who really speaks like this) was that Red Hook, as we had known it, only existed in traces. Mystique is of our own invention and the reasons for its passing are as hard to put a finger on as the expiration date of erotic love. One only knows that it's gone.

As reluctant as I was to admit it outright, I began to have the gnawing feeling that the best days (or rather, nights) of Sunny's were behind the bar as well—thoughts that usually came to me as I drove home in the early mornings, stopping and getting out of my car to feed and address a few of the many feral cats that came out to the streets at that hour. The bar carried Sunny's name but no longer quite his principles, woolly as they were, which had always prized the unplanned and uncalculated. His managerial style most closely resembled a game of pickup sticks: throw the ingredients skyward and let the night fall where it may. While musicians still trekked to Sunny's in great numbers, their appearances were now earnestly promoted, the old bar billed as a venue. One was dissuaded from singing atop the bar or using a booth bench as a platform in order to make a horn better heard over the crowd. Tony, the downcast cowboy with the azure eyes, was forbidden from singing entirely; Tone worried that he would depress the customers (an indictment of the patronage, if there ever was one). And the bagpiper who on St. Patrick's eves past had performed his crisp solitary parade stopped coming on his own.

Dogs were no longer allowed entry, as health inspectors seemed always to be waiting around the nearest corner to enforce their gloomy laws, and the lone feline regular, a white tomcat named Icarus who had on many nights stood by the front door, a sentinel as loyal as Gunga Din, while his owner drank inside, disappeared, too, perhaps sensing that he wasn't welcome anymore. It's an ominous development for any bar when its most illustrious customers start turning tail.

A trip to Sunny's had always been something of a convergence of present and past. And, at its best moments, of reality and unreality. But in its newest edition, there was a good deal of the former and less and less phantasmagoria. One Friday, two dozen twenty-something-year-olds arrived en masse, brought to the bar doorstep by a party bus, an infernal invention that shuttles its passengers on all-night safaris of bars throughout the city. Buzz, our resident cynic, surveyed the scene and asked me earnestly, "Are we on Spring Break, Tim? Have we been transported to Daytona Beach?" The band of nomadic revelers only stayed for the duration of one round but their brief stopover made its point. Sunny's had become just another place—still one of the most striking bars one is likely to enter, but no longer one that stirs a person to renounce all other bars. The faces that now filled the room were the faces one might see in any number of the many spots that had opened Brooklyn-wide in recent years. And the conversations were conversations one might overhear anywhere. No talk of Johnny Keyholes or Blackjack. There were no Joes either. Nor Bimbo Sisters, Falstaffs, or bug eaters. Even the bilateral hermaphrodite who had arrived on a tricycle one summer to sing "Lydia the Tattooed Lady" was certain to never return. She had moved home to Cleveland, I was told, and was working as a surgeon. Of trees.

IT IS ONLY in hindsight that one divides one's life into periods. The college years. The enlistment years. A first marriage. A second bachelorhood. The happiest time of one's life. A melancholia. Our individual periods overlap historical ones—hot and cold wars, space races and great societies, oil embargoes and cyber ages. A bar, if it exists long enough, experiences eras as well, both its own and the ones the world at large is undergoing. The Balzano family bar was a wine bar in its first manifestation, opened by an aging immigrant named Raffaele and his son-in-law Antonio, both of whom barely spoke English. The era of the two Balzano brothers, John and Ralph, lasted for roughly sixty years. It was a working class bar nearly all of its life but it is no longer one. There was the five-year-long speakeasy period, which came in the middle of the Sunny years. Now, his influence waning and his authority mostly titular, the bar had entered a post-Sunny era.

Then, of course, there were the historical eras that affected not only this bar but all New York bars. The age of Prohibition. The period of the legal eighteen-year-old.

I first came to Sunny's near the end of two other such eras—the final years of the conventional telephone and of the barroom smoker. The passing of both has changed all bars. The ouster of the landline phone by the handheld, intelligent variety has led the solitary drinker to look for company in the glow of a miniature screen instead of their neighboring barstool. Bar bets, too, have suffered as there now is an instant resolution to all disputes of the trivial kind. The proscription on smoking in New York City bars has changed the view, the smell, the sensation of being in a bar—in this case, a tolerable metamorphosis in my view.

I now know that my arrival at Sunny's coincided with the tail end of another period, the final years before the real arrival of the Information Age. The Internet was not yet in wide usage in the mid-nineties and the impulse of the layman to reveal, review, document, or comment upon every existing establishment (and, seemingly, upon every place and subject on earth) did not yet exist. It was still possible to have a secret bar, a secluded neighborhood, a private getaway.

Ken Kesey once said, "The need for mystery is greater than the need for an answer." This is something Sunny might have said and it is something that I believe in. When it comes to a business, it may be sensible to have a listing in the phone book, posted business hours, one's name printed on the awning, a website, and a social media page—all of which Sunny's would eventually adopt—but it's hardly interesting. The less one knows of a place the larger its hold on our imagination, a principle that applies to people as well, which is probably why so many of the stories that Sunny told of his life seemed less accounts than fables. He intuited this and ran his bar accordingly.

One of the other lost virtues of the pre-information age was that one could not preview an experience beforehand. The greatest pleasures, I've decided, are those that come to us by surprise and by our own discovery.

I did in time chance upon another bar, deeper in Brooklyn, a diamond hiding in plain sight, where nobody knew me and all was new. Beneath elevated train tracks and along a particularly grim stretch of avenue where all other businesses within a half-mile in any direction were shuttered at night (in other words, in a highly compelling locale), it was disguised as a very ordinary sort of place. The standard neon beer logos filled the windows and inside, there were television screens galore. At one time known as a "bucket of blood"—that is to say, a notoriously dangerous dive—now its door was watched by a security guard twice the size of an ordinary man, patting down any new arrival possessing a scowl, a penis, or any other shady attribute. Those under thirty weren't allowed entry at all. But the place was full of extravagant personalities, many of whom went by assumed names: Love Man, Silver Fox, Black Velvet, Lady Dante, Cassius Clay, Big Daddy, Dottie Diva, Stickyboy, Sippy, Chango, Lefty, and Ajax. Dressing stylishly was the standard. It was taken for granted that one could play an instrument or sing. Religious observance was prevalent though the demigods here weren't named Williams, Sinatra, Baker, Dorsey, and Waits but Brown and

Cooke, Franklin and Knight, Pendergrass and Vandross. By congregational agreement, one only went one night a week, in this case Sundays—a people after my own convictions.

It wasn't long before I, too, took on a new name and bought myself several suits. I found a regular date and we began going every week. A Belizean DJ with an instinct for showmanship announced each arrival and I can confirm that having one's name called out as if one were a dignitary does a good deal for a person's morale. Drinking was generally of only passing interest here while spontaneous acts of altruism were widespread. Seeing me bareheaded one night, a working cowboy (a misnomer only in the sense that the animals he worked with were equine not bovine) named JR led me out-side and to an alley where an old white Cadillac was parked. He popped the trunk and presented me with a choice of wide-brimmed hats. On another evening, seeing me empty-handed, two brothers named Jacob and Esau presented me with a pair of maracas. "I first heard this song in 1970 in a country called Vietnam," Esau said later that night from the bandstand. "I had been shot up by an AK-47 and as I lay in a hospital recuperating, it seemed the only song they ever played on the radio was this number by Mr. Brook Benton." "Hoverin' by my suitcase, tryin' to find a warm place to spend the night/ Heavy rain fallin', seems I hear your voice callin' 'It's all right,'" he sang, the words so familiar but the pleasure in hearing them from this man made them fresh again. One singer outshone James Brown—and, yes, I know what I'm saying. Another was a master of the David Ruffin high falsetto and the sole practitioner of a shuffle he called the "Norfolk Shuffle." It was, by and large, an older crowd—many in their seventh, eighth, and ninth decades—and the

most senior of all, a woman also named Esau (in my experience, in bars as in Yoknapatawpha County, multiple people
tend to share the same name), recalled for us the time she kept
intimate company with a man named Pinocchio. "Keep lyin',
motherfucker! Keep lyin'!" she'd urged him on like a jockey
exhorting a horse. What a line!

A few of the customers owned actual horses and on note-
worthy occasions, such as Mother's or Valentine's Day, they
brought them along in trailers, taking the most intrepid of
the women for short rides to the next corner and back.
Through the windows one could see the animals neighing in
the dark at the trains rumbling overhead toward Long Island
while people inside danced either the wobble, the dougie, the
step, the cha-cha slide, or attempted the camel walk. It was, as
Sunny surely would have put it, a magnificent juxtaposition
of images, a musical as much as a visual spectacle, but my
involvement ran deeper than that of a mere spectator. I would
soon make many honest friendships here.

Somehow I had come across two singularly sublime bars
in twenty years, each a magic theater, a better record than
most, though only in the first instance was the discovery entirely coincidental. I had, unconsciously, been searching for
something else as my sense of disenchantment grew, like a
man whose marriage is unraveling and who begins looking
around before its actual conclusion. To Tone, a resourceful
and forward-looking person, I had become an obstructionist,
protesting every supposed innovation and every incursion of
modernity. I discreetly shut down the whirring ice machine
whenever possible. I sent a salesman of credit card machinery
packing with a gentle "Get the fuck out of here!" At her suggestion that the bar install an automated teller machine, I

said, "Over my dead body." Fearing that I meant it, Sunny, in his last executive decision, backed me up on this matter while Tone looked at the two of us with an expression that said, "Am I to suffer just because you're allergic to the twenty-first century?" My loyalties and mind divided, I didn't have the resolve after sixteen years to leave on my own volition, intuiting however, that with each dissent I was either digging my own grave or tunneling my way out the back. When it came, the final rift was a mere formality and as I turned the lock that night, I sensed it would be for the last time. Up above, Sunny's windows were dark and though he seemed very far away right then, it was with relief as much as regret that I turned away. There is a corner turned, a direction taken, a door opened and a door closed.

29

All Summer in a Day

A YEAR LATER, THE GREATEST RAIN IN MEMORY ARrived. Sunny and I had often talked of our shared love of storms. He had had a German neighbor once named Jackie Schultz who was in this regard a fellow devotee as well as an opera enthusiast, and when the sky looked promisingly dark, he liked to invite Sunny over and the two would sit, smoking and drinking and listening to Wagner, Brahms, Mozart, and wait for the show to begin. As a young child, I had watched from the windows as well, as the backyards filled with monsoon downpour, each a growing puddle until they connected and joined up with the overflowing rice paddies and all of the outdoors became to my eyes an inland sea. When the clouds dried up, I would navigate its waters in a red plastic washtub, admiral of infinite space, or so it seemed. In West Africa, the lights usually went out at the first thunderclap. Our roof was flat and double-layered and an outer shell of corrugated aluminum would create a deafening percussion throughout the house when the rains of short-lived downpours drummed down on it. The rains in Europe weren't violent in degree but unending. The sky was often overcast for weeks, once memorably drizzling daily for more than fifty days, and the broad Rhine would rise over its banks and lap up into the ancient towns that lay on both sides, nothing more than fledgling floods that enveloped benches and trees and a few forgotten cars. Even college in Ohio provided the occasional respectable squall, the farming plains a playing field for dueling thunderclaps.

This storm would be nothing like those previous ones, though, all the constituent parts magnified many-fold. In Red Hook, nudged by wind and tugged by tide, the ocean approached the bar from the south, licking up the street and covering the distance from the shoreline to the tires of Sunny's Willys in a few hours. It climbed the stoop and, finding the door locked and sandbagged, pushed its way through the basement windows. Once inside, it was a short leap to mount the stairs and seep between the floorboards like a drink spilling upward and rise three feet up the side of the bar before retreating.

I saw none of this. I hadn't returned to Sunny's or Red Hook, other than to pick Sunny himself up once or twice for doctor appointments, in a year and a month. But the day after the storm's last remnants blew out of town, I drove down spontaneously and, old disagreements forgotten, spent the afternoon along with many other volunteers wading in the unlit basement, raking debris and pumping sludgy water. Nearly all the family history and much of that of the bar, written in documents and photographs and barware long forgotten, had been stored—put away for a rainy day, so to speak—in two adjoining dirt basements and had disintegrated into a murky soup. There was no time for sentimentality and whatever was still solid was carried out to enormous demolition dumpsters. The bar would close for a year, and Sunny's family endured a winter without hot water or electricity. Newspaper reporters and camera crews, local and from as far away as Europe, converged for the human interest angle. The rebuilding would cost many thousands of dollars and fundraisers, both virtual and the traditional kind, were held. "Sunny's must be saved!" went the battle cry. The flood had weakened the foundations both of the bar and, out of the public eye, of Sunny and Tone's marriage, an improbable union to begin with. Quietly and without lasting ill will, they separated as a wedded couple, making their upstairs/downstairs living arrangement a permanent resolution. At his age and in his weakened state, Sunny could contribute little to the actual rebuilding of the bar, which took place all around him, turning his attention instead on improving his guitar skills. His self-taught style resembled Django Reinhardt's—his fingers, while not actually paralyzed, too thick for traditional guitar techniques. No one ever accused Sunny of practicality and art had always brought him solace in times of anxiety. On a leaky ship, he would sooner begin a new canvas than patch the hole—an apt metaphor perhaps for his romantic life as well. He abandoned any pretense of sobriety as well, contending that his life was his own and he no longer had to answer to anyone, putting out of mind the notion that parenthood late in life comes with some basic expectations of temperance.

When it came time at each fundraising gala for the honored guest to make an appearance, Sunny would be ushered onto the stage, more of a figurehead than ever. "I feel like General MacArthur out here," he once said, a reference, I was certain, that no one understood. He had taken to wearing a rakish fedora. At one such event, held at a large concert hall, he said a few misty-eyed words and then told an indecent joke (indecent if you were either Irish or a woman). The crowd applauded hesitantly, a trace of condescension unmistakably in the air by those who had never really known him. In the green room afterward, he said to me, "I'm so touched by all these people who have given what it is that it is they're giving. But the truth is, Timmy, they may think they're doing it for me but they're doing it for themselves. I could have lived without the bar ever coming back. It's had its time, a beautiful time, just like those sand mandalas that the Tibetan monks create. Aye?"

The bar did reopen to fanfare and one can now go six days a week if one likes. It's a vibrant sort of place. The crowd is generally young and there is music nearly every night. On Saturdays, a bluegrass jam. I returned a few times, not staying for longer than two beers, the sense of displacement never entirely subsiding. One early Sunday evening, Bobby, the founder of the Brooklyn Stage Company, one of the few people who remained from my earliest days there, four years sober now, put on the one-act Eugene O'Neill play *Hughie* in the bar. He played the role of the lead character himself and it was a marvelous rendition—one of those performances that spoils any future productions of the play one might see. As I watched Bobby pacing up and down the bar, holding forth, actor and character one and the same to me, I thought to myself that Sunny's still exists as an inspirational place, if not for me, then for others. I accepted this with nothing but serenity.

SUNNY HAD NEVER seemed to care what people thought of him, a valuable trait undoubtedly made easier to sustain by his knowledge that he was widely revered. He had fewer regrets than most people; after all, his favorite phrase was, "I yam what I yam and that's all I yam." He squandered some talents, his artistic ones perhaps, and made the most of others. The ones that leave lasting impressions. His gift for gab as well as guidance, both imparted so eloquently, his hospitality, his grace. I know he is still spoken of, and most fondly, by the many people who in time have passed through and possibly by some that have passed on, life and afterlife differing only in that two-way conversations are exclusive to the former. He could be loyal and libertine, sometimes migrainous in his stubbornness and his foolish addictions. I admire him to no end for being the most original man I have ever met.

Sunny once presided over a wedding held on a nearby river barge and later at the bar. The bride, an artist named Jen, was an ethereal woman, exquisite in all the important ways, and he was understandably as taken by her as was the groom. "There are paintings that are representations of women," he said to me later. "But I look at this woman and I see a representation of a painting." When I think of Sunny this way, as a painting of a man, it's not Rembrandt or Titian or Close or his beloved Picasso that come to mind but Jackson Pollock. A different man to different people, interpretable in countless ways, no interpretation more true than any others. This is mine.

Acknowledgments

An editor's intuition and guidance are as invisible to the reader as gravity but, in my experience, no less profound. My deepest thanks to Noah Eaker for his indefatigable optimism, candor, forbearance, and friendship. I have been singularly fortunate and I know it. Also, to Maria Massie, my literary agent and steadfast personal advocate—thank you!

A book's creation begins long before the first word is written. Over the years the following people have, knowingly or not, provided counsel, loyal support, critical thinking, and uncritical camaraderie: John Pinamonti, Marianna Baer, Gabriel Cohen, Isaura Horenstein, Tone Johansen, Charles Bradley, Larose Jackson, Julie and Chris Cummings, Robert Francis Cole, Christopher and Antje Croton, Emily Votruba, Mark Adams, Sara Lippmann, James Linville, Francis Kerrigan, Louise Bauso, Sarah Welch, Rachel Schulder, Griffith and Sterling Iffith, Scott Murchison, Julie Qashu, Michael C. Maronna, Keith Romer, Jenny Witherell, Bill McBride, Frank Buffa, Jim Sucich, Robert and Annie Del Principe, Ralph Hassard, Bob and Rachel Prince, Pete Waldman,

Jimmy Hill, Dorothy Lofton, Randy Gaffney, Denise Jones, Jason Elias, Meg Willett, Arietta Venizelos, and Christine Krol. A deep bow to Osamu Koyama, at whose sushi counter many of these pages were written, and to early supporters Laura Ford and Daniel Menaker, as well as the staff of the Brooklyn Collection at the Brooklyn Public Library.

The Poisoner's Handbook by Deborah Blum, The Black Hand by Thomas Pitkin, and Sidney T. Smith's 1942 study The Red Hook Section of Brooklyn all made essential contributions to this book, and I thank these authors for their diligence.

About the Author

TIM SULTAN's work has appeared in *The New York Times, The Spectator,* and *GQ.* The son of a Foreign Service officer, he was raised abroad in Laos, the Ivory Coast, and Germany. He is a graduate of Kenyon College and lives in New York City, where he works as an urban gardener.

About the Type

This book was set in Garamond, a typeface originally designed by the Parisian type cutter Claude Garamond (c. 1500–61). This version of Garamond was modeled on a 1592 specimen sheet from the Egenolff-Berner foundry, which was produced from types assumed to have been brought to Frankfurt by the punch cutter Jacques Sabon (c. 1520–80).

Claude Garamond's distinguished romans and italics first appeared in *Opera Ciceronis* in 1543–44. The Garamond types are clear, open, and elegant.